Contents

ADVANCE PRAISE FOR
PASSION PROJECTS FOR SMART PEOPLE

"A book that celebrates and demonstrates creativity … unfailingly positive."
—*Foreword Reviews*

"Every science teacher with a pair of hiking boots should read this book!"
—**Chris McKay**, NASA planetary scientist

"This up-beat, can-do book is delightful to read and energizes you to get up and out to learn and teach science. The book is a guide that provides much practical advice on where to start and become involved in a myriad of ways to make the world a better place, and have fun too! The book has great detail with step by step guidance on how to maximize opportunities, where to seek support and how to cultivate your passions."
—**Sarah Allen**, Ph.D., wildlife biologist

"**Passion Projects for Smart People** is inspiring! Its proposals of interesting ventures and its profiles of dynamic individuals will be motivating to anyone seeking a greater sense of accomplishment and fulfillment in their lives."
—**David R. Lapp**, physics teacher, Tamalpais High School and author of *The Physics of Music and Musical Instruments*

"Dr. Wing is a smart man with diverse experience following his passions. His easy-to-read book is full of relatable anecdotes and practical information for anyone looking to pursue a more enriching life."
—**Joe Stewart**, high school science teacher leader

PASSION PROJECTS FOR SMART PEOPLE

Turn Your Intellectual Pursuits into Fun, Profit, and Recognition

Michael R. Wing, Ph.D.

Fresno, California

Main cover image courtesy Mc Satori/Shutterstock
Additional images: www.publicdomainpictures.net
and pixabay.com

Published by Quill Driver Books
An imprint of Linden Publishing
2006 South Mary Street, Fresno, California 93721
(559) 233-6633 / (800) 345-4447
QuillDriverBooks.com

Quill Driver Books and Colophon are trademarks of
Linden Publishing, Inc.

ISBN 978-1-61035-306-9

135798642

Printed in the United States of America
on acid-free paper.

Library of Congress Cataloging-in-Publication Data on file.

Introduction

This is the story of a ninth grade teacher who learned to do more with the resources he already had. He did field work in the Galapagos, Costa Rica, Alaska, Finland, Namibia, India, the United Arab Emirates, the Pacific Ocean and the high Arctic, with outside organizations paying his way. He published in peer-reviewed journals, won grants from corporations and the National Geographic Society, and collaborated with organizations like NASA, the University of California, and the National Park Service. His projects range from marine biology to high altitude gardening, astrobiology, to archaeology. It took time for him to discover opportunities that were hiding in plain sight. One project would lead to another. Doing projects made him more creative. Along the way he met other people who use ordinary resources to do remarkable things. That teacher was me, and my life is richer now.

Where do I find the time? I can afford to move ahead slowly on my own projects since they're not my primary source of income. I spend only a few hours most weeks on all of these activities put together. Most of my time goes to my students and my family. My students participate in these extracurricular projects, and as my own children get more involved in them, my family is starting to benefit, too. But really I do them for my own personal satisfaction. I love coming to work in the morning. I can't retire; I would lose the affiliation with my school that makes some of these projects possible.

It sounds like extra work for no pay, but besides the fun of doing them, projects sometimes lead to extra earnings and opportunities. Once you become an expert on something, you can get hired for consulting services. You can teach a class. You may become eligible for free travel and conferences. You may write a book that makes money. The people I have profiled in this book earn money in all of these ways, and so do I. Most years I supervise a class at my school for advanced students called "independent science research" in addition to my full-time regular teaching, and I am paid thousands of extra dollars for doing that. If you are a teacher, you may want to look into this possibility with your district. I also often get to travel for free to interesting places.

I've met people who exemplify this lifestyle in different ways. A few are school teachers like me but there are also other working professionals, retirees, and stay-at-home parents. Their areas of expertise include the natural sciences, anthropology, history, and the arts. What they all have in common is projects that started small but got traction. The payoffs were life-altering. They have ongoing projects, institutional affiliations, and collaborators. They apply for grants and apply to participate in programs. They travel with professional purpose and often they get someone else to pay for it. They mentor others and publish what they've done for posterity. You can do these things, too. The following chapters give specific examples, from my own and other people's experiences.

1

Have Projects

"If you have built castles in the air, your work need not be lost; that is where they should be. Now put the foundations under them."
—Henry David Thoreau, *Walden*

The people in this book have projects which are long-term, creative, and original: things nobody has done before. They think about their projects often, even when they're not working on them, and that adds meaning to their lives and gives them satisfaction. The French have a related concept—"le jardin secret" (the secret garden)—that most often describes an extramarital affair. This book is not about how to do that. Still, having an absorbing but part-time project to occupy your waking thoughts is sort of like having a romantic affair. To live like these people do, you need at least one ongoing project.

Where does the inspiration for an original project come from? Louis Pasteur once said that chance favors the prepared mind. You need experience. My best ideas come to me on a long vigorous hike, or while traveling to a new place, or otherwise doing something a bit outside of my comfort zone. They are stimulated by conversations with creative people. They are often syntheses of two or more ideas, observations, or problems that previously appeared to be unrelated. They arise from projects I am already doing. The ideas do not come to me during my daily work/life routine, so I have to get outside of that framework. It can help to keep a notebook or the electronic equivalent; you will find yourself running for it because all the good stuff will occur to you when you don't have it on your person. Here are some stories about projects we do at my school that illustrate the apparently random way that chance can favor the prepared mind:

A horticulture project

All schools have an occasional speaker from the outside world. It pays to invite the speaker to lunch afterwards. My school was visited by an expert on Mars, Dr. Pascal Lee of the Mars Institute, who showed us slides of his research camp on Devon Island, in Canada's high Arctic. He goes there because the landforms and climate make it similar to the Red Planet. He loves it, and seeing his presentation made us want to go there too. In an unguarded moment during lunch, Dr. Lee invited us to get involved. I started to try to think of a Mars-colony type of high school project to build there: A greenhouse? (They already have one.) A composting toilet? An Arctic chicken coop?

Our slender budget wasn't going to get anyone from my school to Devon Island anyway, since the cost of transporting one person there and back with supplies is in the low five figures. I kept in touch with Dr. Lee but felt stymied. (Since then I have made the trip twice, once catching a free training flight with the New York Air National Guard that Pascal arranged and once on a National Geographic Society Waitt grant that I obtained by myself.)

A year after Dr. Lee's visit I was touring the Galapagos as part of a study tour for teachers (the Toyota International Teacher Program) and saw a demonstration farm run by Carlos Zapata on Isla Santa Cruz. It bothered Mr. Zapata that as the population of the islands grew, all the food was imported. Most of the islands' area is national park, but the remaining bit has fertile volcanic soils, adequate rain, and can grow anything. He built the farm to produce local vegetables and to show that his island can live sustainably. Seeing his farm reminded me of Devon Island, and of some other remote scientific field stations I knew about. I remembered having hiked past the University of California's White Mountain Research Station at an elevation of 12,500 feet on the California/Nevada border and I thought: "We'll grow food there. It's cheaper to get to than Devon Island, and almost as cold." I am sure I would never have had the idea if I hadn't seen Mr. Zapata's farm, if I hadn't previously hiked in the White Mountains, and if Dr. Lee had not come to our school.

The management of the White Mountain Research Station gave me the go-ahead the same day I pitched my idea to them. They have always been helpful and accommodating to us, and this is a lesson I have learned about research institutions: They want to help schools. They just don't know how.

Sir Francis Drake High School's alpine cold frame at the University of California's White Mountain Research Station (elevation of 12,470'). It is the highest garden in North America. Photo by Michael Wing.

When a secondary school teacher approaches a university, government lab, museum, or other non-school institution with a specific request, the answer is often "yes."

Our school's parent fund gave several thousand dollars to pursue this unusual idea. My principal was supportive. A group of students and I built a four-foot by eight-foot cold frame (a miniature greenhouse) during the winter at school, and we installed it on the mountain the following summer. Over the years we added an automatic hydraulic ventilation system, and solar-powered electrical and irrigation systems. My science department colleague Cooper Clark and I have led more than a dozen trips to the White Mountains since then, bringing over fifty students, parents, and teachers from our school. Most of those students and parents have participated in multiple trips over several years. The project attracted $20,000 in corporate grants from outside the school. We have successfully grown radishes, potatoes, salad greens, winter wheat, garlic, and herbs. We plant in the spring, harvest in the fall, and the system automatically looks after itself the rest of the time. For seven years it was the highest altitude garden in America. We took it down recently.

When we travel to the White Mountains we sleep and eat at the University of California's Crooked Creek facility, a big, comfortable lodge at ten thousand feet with a caretaker and cook. This place isn't open to the public. It's for graduate students and professors while they're in the mountains doing research. We're the only high school that uses the facility, mainly because we're the only high school that has asked.

Maybe we grew the most expensive radishes in the world, but our purpose was educational and experimental. Most of the students involved in the project have gone on to study science or engineering in college. One of them is now getting her Ph.D. in geophysics at Stanford. The local newspaper, the *Marin Independent Journal*, wrote a front-page article about us. The project gave me credibility when I applied for programs and grants. The point of this story is not that other people should build gardens on mountaintops. The point is that novel projects can pay off unexpectedly, and that collaboration with others and the synthesis of unrelated ideas and experiences lead to novel projects.

The project did not result in a paper in a scientific journal. It was an amateur engineering project, not a proper science experiment. The plants grew well but we didn't have good control over the temperature and humidity in the growth chambers because we weren't there most of the time. There were way too many variables and too many unexpected setbacks, like the time we had a hard frost in early August that burst a valve, or the time a marmot got in. We started to look around on White Mountain Peak for a way to do some real science, and that wasn't hard to find.

A trees project

Near the research station are two groves of bristlecone pines, which are known for being the oldest trees in the world. They are famous from postcards and Sierra Club calendar illustrations because of their stark beauty. They live higher than other trees, at elevations of nine to eleven thousand feet. On mature trees much of the trunk is bare, and the exposed wood gets sandblasted to a light brown color by windblown ice crystals. Some trees are mostly dead, with just a thin strip of living bark connecting the roots to a single dark green branch. We always pay several visits to these groves whenever we go to the White Mountains.

Spiral grain detail in bristlecone pines (*Pinus longaeva*) in California's White Mountains. Photo by Michael Wing.

The grain in the wood is not straight. Some trees twist like corkscrews, and we noticed that the spiral grain (in the language of forestry) can be either right-handed or left-handed. However, most of the time the grain has gentle curves but does not spiral strongly. We asked an expert on bristlecone pines why they twist, and she told us no one knows. This surprised us, so we read up on the arcane subject of spiral grain in conifers, which isn't limited to bristlecone pines. Most of the articles we read were written by forestry professionals, for whom spiral grain is a nuisance. It makes the timber less valuable.

We learned there are a number of schools of thought on the origin of spiral grain. Prevailing winds, the Coriolis effect, and the movement of the sun across the sky have all been invoked. Perhaps spiral grain helps distribute water evenly between the tree's roots and the crown, or perhaps it strengthens the trunk against breakage. Some have proposed that spiral grain relieves growth stresses in the bark caused by cell division. Or, maybe it's "just" genetics; like handedness in humans.

A lot of the explanations we read didn't address the left- vs. right-handed question, and some were not consistent with our observation that left-handed trees are more common than right-handed ones. We realized that we had an opportunity to test some of these hypotheses in the field, especially the ones that invoked environmental conditions. We made a big data table in Excel. Over the course of two years we measured ten parameters on each of six hundred trees in two distinct groves. We had to give each team of students a right-handed wine corkscrew to carry so they could distinguish between left-handed and right-handed trees, because the thin air at 11,000 feet makes it difficult to think straight. The results were clear: The proportion of left-handed, right-handed, and "straight" trees is exactly the same in every part of every grove we looked at, and not at all correlated with elevation, exposure, tree size, slope angle, or anything else. Maybe it's just genetics.

Some of my students submitted this work at our local science fair, and it got favorable attention from the judges. The student who did the statistics on this project went on to the regional and state science fairs and won a special prize at the California State Fair: the Mu Alpha Theta Award for the "most challenging, thorough and creative investigation of a problem involving mathematics accessible to a high school student." Since some of the academic papers I had read to get started were published in the Springer-Verlag journal *Trees: Structure and Function,* we wrote up our results in their format and submitted it. They published it! (Wing M.R., Knowles A.J., Melbostad S.R., and Jones A.K., [2014]; "Spiral grain in bristlecone pines (*Pinus longaeva*) exhibits no correlation with environmental factors." *Trees: Structure and Function* Volume 28, Number 2, pages 487–491.) Not bad, since none of us had ever studied trees before and we had no outside help from any tree expert. We had found some low-hanging fruit (an unresolved question) and we picked it. But this could not have happened if we hadn't already been doing an unrelated project, our garden, in the White Mountains.

This project is finished, but we still like to visit the bristlecone pines. The first-year female cones of this species are dark purple on most trees but on some trees they are yellow-green. "A genetic variation" is the customary explanation. That's all anybody knows about it. No one appears to have measured the ratio of purple to green. Does it vary from place to place? We still have our global positioning system receivers, clipboards, and willing students. We're planning another big survey.

A microbiology project

We call a third project we're doing in the White Mountains our artificial hypoliths project. This one started when a few years ago I signed up for a NASA professional development program for teachers and graduate students called Spaceward Bound. A planetary scientist, Dr. Chris McKay, took us into the Mojave Desert to show us how communities of bacteria and algae survive this environment, hidden under rocks and salt crusts, and even inside of them. He is interested in this topic because he helps NASA decide where on Mars to look for hidden forms of life.

I met Chris McKay and learned about his program through a series of lucky accidents. Pascal Lee mentioned his name to me so I made an appointment to discuss the high altitude garden. It was in the early stages of the project, and I was still figuring out what direction to take it. On the day of the appointment, he wasn't in his office at the NASA Ames Research Center. Some kind of complicated emergency had come up. I wasn't the only person looking for him; as I stood outside the open door of his office, every few minutes somebody would come down the hall, look through the doorway, and say, "Where's Chris?" "I don't know" I would say, as if I belonged there. There was a poster on the wall about a trip to Axel Heiberg Island, in the high Arctic. It looked like one of the participants was a middle school teacher. In the conference room next door several people were having a heated discussion about how to configure a spectrometer that was going to Mars. I eavesdropped, and I actually understood some of what they were saying. An officer of the Mars Society came in to look for Chris. I told her who I was and why I was waiting. "Oh," she said, "Chris should take you on one of his expeditions." That got my attention—he takes teachers on expeditions? I left that day still not having met Chris, but with the name of the person who coordinated the program. I also had a long talk with one of his colleagues about why there are so few organic molecules in Martian soil.

In the Mojave, we would pick up small quartz rocks from the desert floor and turn them over. A green film of cyanobacteria would cover the underside. Here were bacteria you could actually see! As a high school teacher that fact, that you could see the bacteria without a microscope, impressed me. The colonized rocks are called "hypoliths," which means "under rocks" in Greek. Cyanobacteria like living under translucent rocks because there they are protected from drying out from the harsh ultraviolet rays of the sun and from temperature extremes. The rocks act like greenhouse windows, letting through a little sunlight and trapping a little moisture so the microorganisms can do photosynthesis. Back in the White Mountains on one of our trips, I saw that the dry alpine meadows above our research station also have hypoliths.

I decided we would grow our own hypoliths to see how long it takes for the green film to form. I bought some 2 inch square kitchen tiles in three different materials; glass, white marble, and travertine. Since it was for a school project, the tile store sold them to me at cost. The glass tiles transmit over 50 percent of the sunlight that hits their upper surfaces, the marble tiles transmit 5 percent, and the travertine tiles are totally opaque. In the classroom I had students lightly sand their surfaces to remove the polish and engrave their names on the tiles. Chris McKay was going to Namibia, and he invited me along! I placed sixty tiles in the Namib Desert. I even had a student make a ceramic plaque in the school's pottery studio that says "Do Not Disturb—Experiment in Progress."

In the years since then, I or one of my students or school colleagues or NASA colleagues have placed similar arrays of tiles in the White Mountains, the Mojave Desert, the United Arab Emirates, Svalbard, Australia, India, Chile, and on Devon and Cornwallis Islands in Canada's high Arctic. Each of these locations already has natural hypoliths growing there, and I have since been back (or at least have a plan to get back) to all of them, except the set in the United Arab Emirates, to give them a checkup. Their undersides are starting to get colonized, but they are not bright green yet. This takes longer than a few years. We also have a set in Antarctica's Taylor Valley. That set was placed at my request by a middle school teacher and a professor from Arizona, Justin Kendhammer and Egbert Schwartz, who were going there for another purpose.

While in these places I also did a light transmission study, using borrowed NASA equipment, on the natural hypoliths we found there. It shows that cyanobacteria can survive on as little as one-tenth of 1 percent of the sun's direct rays. This work has been published (with co-authors from NASA and South African universities) in the *Journal of Geophysical Research*. The results from the artificial hypoliths are going to be published in an academic journal too, but not until they are bright green, which will take more years. Meanwhile, we check on them from time to time, photographing the undersides of the tiles.

How did I pay for these trips? The Mojave and the White Mountains can be reached on a couple of tanks of gasoline, which is well within my personal budget. NASA generously covered my expenses on the ground in Namibia and the Emirates, since I was traveling with NASA scientists in a program called Spaceward Bound, and I paid for my own airfare by doing some creative scrounging with leftover grant monies from the cold frame project. (If you are a Tamalpais Union High School District budget person reading this, I'm just kidding!) Sometimes I paid for my airfare out of my own pocket. When I went to India with Spaceward Bound, I paid for the whole trip myself, but I used a portion of my stipend from teaching the independent science research class, not my base salary. So in a way, one of my extra-curricular projects was paying for another. My first Arctic trip was on a free Air National Guard training flight. My second Arctic trip was paid for through a National Geographic Society grant I applied for myself and was awarded. The Svalbard array was put there by a former student, Alexander Curth, who is now in college and was doing a semester abroad in Svalbard, so he paid for that one. I mailed the Australia array to a colleague who lives there; he deployed it for me. A NASA colleague brought some tiles to Chile's Atacama Desert.

I could never have started the hypoliths project without Dr. McKay, who taught me the little I know about cyanobacteria. Thanks, Dr. McKay, for mentoring me and taking me with you to three continents! Using the tiles was my own idea though, and I have traveled to many of the hypolith locations without his involvement. I know less than my NASA colleagues about hypoliths, but I was able to think of something original to do that complemented their work. So having an outsider's perspective can be an advantage. Constraints can be an advantage, too. Compared to my colleagues at NASA, I have very little time or money to spend on studying hypoliths. I needed a project that was cheap and easy. But, I can afford to wait years, even decades, to obtain results. Many professionals don't have that luxury.

A history/archaeology project

Another project outside my area of expertise that my students and I are doing involves archaeology. If you know anything about archaeology, alarm bells should be ringing in your head now because it's a field that's unforgiving to amateurs. For good reason: archaeological sites are the ultimate non-renewable resource. You can't just dig wherever you want; you will ruin a site for the rest of time, be labeled a "pot hunter," and probably get yourself arrested. You could even go to jail. Excavating requires a permit, and only a respected professional with a good track record is going to be issued one. PLEASE, if you are not a professional archaeologist, don't ever think about excavating or collecting archaeological artifacts.

So how can I do it? As Indiana Jones once said, most of archaeology is done in the library. A lot of the rest is really surveying: measuring surface features like stones or holes in the ground using non-invasive techniques. I learned this in Finland on a National Science Foundation program for teachers called PolarTREC. We were studying 6,000-year-old hunter-gatherers. The archaeologists I was there with were at the top of their field. They dug an occasional test pit, but they spent most of their time surveying, testing soil chemistry, and making maps. This was partly because the soil in northern Finland is so acidic that everything corrodes away and in most places nothing is left anyway but stone flakes and charcoal. Bone, wood, leather, or shells don't survive there. It was also because the prehistoric people constructed large pit houses and even though the houses had completely rotted away the pits were still visible in the ground. The soil tests were for phosphorus. Even after thousands of years, if people had lived there, the soil phosphorus concentrations were elevated because they ate so much meat and seafood.

After I got home I learned about a strange line of stones in Marin County, where I live. It is on public land. Very little has been written about it. Local historians seem to think it might be prehistoric and some archaeologists think it's historic, so it falls through the cracks. It is 800 feet long, made of granite boulders. It is obviously manmade. It is not a stone wall; it is more like a series of stepping stones with gaps in between them. Many of the stones are too big for one or two people to move without mechanical help. The ends of the lines are distinct.

I was surprised to learn about the site because I had hiked right past it more than once without noticing it. It is hard to see because many of the stones are set into the earth at ground level and because about thirty feet of the line are missing where the trail (an old ranch road) intersects it. It is not shown on any public maps. It can have no practical use. It is too low to serve as a fence for livestock. A cow can easily walk across it, or pass around the ends.

Some people call it the Spirit Jumping-Off Rocks and tell a story about why the Coast Miwok people built it, but opinion on this is divided. There aren't any other structures like it that are attributed to the Miwok.

Nevertheless, somebody put it there and invested a lot of work doing it. It does not mark a property line today, and apparently it never did. You can tell it's been there a long time. The rocks are completely covered in lichens and we know they were there before 1862, because the line appears on a government survey map made that year. The first Anglo-American rancher, Solomon Pierce, obtained the land just four years earlier. Pierce was from Vermont. Did he start to lay out a Vermont-style stone wall and then lose interest? Was it Pierce's folly? It's hard to understand doing that in your first few years on the land; you would think he would have had more pressing business to attend to.

Besides Solomon Pierce and the Coast Miwok there are other groups who have had the opportunity to build the line, from the paleo-Indians ten thousand years ago to the Russian fur hunters to the Mexican-period ranchers. This part of California has a surprisingly rich history. The problem was to figure out who did build it, and why.

My students and I interviewed historians, archaeologists, and ranchers to find out what they knew. Different people told us different things. Then we took the same approach we did with the bristlecone pines: We surveyed the line, measured a bunch of different parameters on each stone (there are about 700 stones in the line), and put it all into a giant spreadsheet. The measurements were done with meter sticks, a measuring tape, and global positioning system receivers. We didn't even have to touch the stones to do the survey. For comparison purposes, we also examined stone walls in our area that we know were built by ranchers.

A statistical analysis of the stones and their orientations and spacing was very revealing. Whoever built the line had placed large stones lengthwise and small stones crosswise to maintain a constant width of half a meter. This is something New England stone wall builders do. There is a ten meter gap in the line where the old ranch road crosses it, but there aren't enough extra stones in the area to plug the gap. It looks like the gap was planned from the beginning. Plus, the line changes direction at the gap so as to intersect the head of a steep ravine. Historic wooden fence posts can be found at either end of the line. A pile of unused stones lies hidden in the bushes near the northern end.

It all points to the line having been built by ranchers, either as a property boundary or a stone wall that was never finished. We took our draft report to the park's archaeologist and he agreed with our conclusions. We argued that the park should interpret the stone line to the public, and they have

PASSION PROJECTS FOR SMART PEOPLE

started to move forward on that. A newspaper, the Pulitzer Prize–winning *Point Reyes Light,* did a feature article on our project. We gave a copy of our report to the state Office of Historic Preservation's Northwest Information Center. Now anyone who is curious about the line in the future can find our study there. We submitted our report to a peer-reviewed academic journal and after some back-and-forth reviews and revisions they published it. (Wing M.R., Iida K. and Wearing E., [2015] "Stone-by-stone metrics shed new light on a unique stone alignment at the Point Reyes National Seashore, Marin County, Alta California." *California Archaeology.* Vol. 7, No. 2. pp. 245–264.) That experience has been an education in itself. At one point we were advised by a prominent archeologist to change our conclusions to avoid angering a local Indian tribe. Yet, the tribal leaders themselves have been honest enough to say "we just don't know" and have shown very little interest in our study. So probably in a few years, hikers will find an interpretive plaque at the trailhead detailing everything that is and is not known about the line.

Our study shows the fun you can have measuring old structures. There are probably some overlooked ones near you. Ask around. Just make sure you have a permit. We found out after the fact that we should have applied to the park service for one, even though we were just looking at the stones.

Now that we've done this I have started to notice other outdoor history features in my local landscape that tell stories about the past. Besides stone walls, there are some old lime kilns, mines, and quarries. The streams here frequently have ruined foundations of small dams, probably left over from when each neighborhood had its own water district. Redwood stumps are present in many places from logging operations over a century ago—I even have one in my backyard. You can tell from the diameter of the stumps whether it was old growth or not. You can estimate from the diameters of the new trees that sprout from the stumps how long it's been since the cutting. Ranches in my area have left behind old orchards of non-native pear, apple, and plum trees, rose bushes, flowering bulbs, and huge eucalyptus trees that persist for generations after the buildings are gone. There are some semi-neglected cemeteries from the nineteenth and early twentieth centuries with only a few grave markers in each. There are Indian morteros, cavities in the bedrock where Miwok women used to grind acorns and seeds. In the back of my mind there is an idea for a book called *Decoding the Landscape,* an inventory and atlas of these outdoor features in Marin County, California. Compared with the historic buildings, they get almost no attention from anyone. I have dibs on Marin County! But there are over 3,000 other counties in the United States, so it would seem that this book could be written many, many times. Plus, in the White Mountains where we have our other projects, there are many stone structures above the tree line. Some are prehistoric, some historic. There are hunting blinds, tent circles, shepherd's huts, sheep corrals, and food caches. Can we learn to tell the difference? Most of them are just low rings or horseshoe-shaped piles of rocks. The prehistoric Indian sites are already well documented, but it appears nobody has paid much attention to the rest. This one could take many years.

· ·

Profile: D. S. (Dewey) Livingston, historian

Dewey Livingston is one of the people we consulted about the "Spirit Jumping-Off Rocks." As a professional historian, an expert on early ranches in our area, and a local resident, he knows as much as anybody does about them. Surprisingly, Dewey does not have a degree in history. He has no college degree. He is self-trained, and also received training when he worked for the National Park Service as a historical technician. Nevertheless, he has published more than a dozen history books and technical reports totaling thousands of pages, and has earned his living doing it. His work has practical importance, too, since much of it consists of historic resource studies for the National Park Service. The Park Service uses his documents to guide management decisions about the historical buildings and other features in the parks, and to develop interpretive programs. Millions of visitors to some of our most popular Western parks benefit indirectly from his work.

As a young man Dewey worked at a variety of jobs in the Bay Area and near his hometown of Inverness, California. He got his start in history by knocking at the door of Jack Mason, a retired newspaper editor, historian, and neighbor. In his retirement Jack Mason published eight books and a quarterly history journal. He also started a local history museum in the parlor of his house. Dewey offered to help Jack out with his projects, and as he gained experience and Jack became ill, they gradually reversed roles. When Jack Mason died, his historic house was purchased by the Inverness Foundation for use as the local library and also as a museum to hold his collection of maps, photographs, books, artifacts, and other documents.

The Jack Mason Museum of West Marin History was launched, with Dewey as its volunteer historian.

The Point Reyes National Seashore needed a historical technician and hired Dewey on the strength of his experience working with Jack Mason. He worked there for ten years doing historic resource studies. After that, he quit his job with the Park Service but continued to do the same work as a consultant. His jobs for the Park Service have taken him to Death Valley, the Channel Islands, the Mojave National Preserve, and parks in Arizona, Nevada, and Hawaii. A historic resource study is a (frequently) telephone book-size report that documents everything known about the history and cultural significance of a site. Dewey's reports are very readable. Their lyrical titles hint at the stories they have to tell: *A good life: dairy farming in the Olema Valley: a history of the dairy and beef ranches of the Olema Valley and Lagunitas Canyon, Golden Gate National Recreation Area* is one. *On the Pacific Horizon: Five Islands within Channel Islands National Park* is another. Today, work comes to him. Dewey attributes his success to his skillful use of a local historian's perspective within the academic and technical constraints on this type of work. "I kind of blended the amateur's eye for detail with the professional standards," he says.

Although work for the Park Service has been his bread and butter, Dewey also writes commercial books, prepares nominations for the National Register of Historic Places, and does oral history projects. In our area, various cities and towns are turning one hundred years old, or have done so recently, although the histories of these places go back much further than that. The Nicasio Historical Society contracted Dewey to write a book about Nicasio, California, on the occasion of its centennial. Kentfield (my home town) has done the same, and as I spoke with Dewey I learned he had interviews of elderly neighbors of mine who live on my street. Dewey has also published a book through Arcadia Publishing's *Images of America* series. It is mostly historical photographs. The Point Reyes National Seashore Association published his pamphlet *Discovering Historic Ranches at Point Reyes.*

Dewey is ambivalent about not having a university degree: "Did I lose something by not having it? Or, would it be suffocating?" he muses. "Because I have no complaints about the work I'm doing!" It seems that in the Park Service, the higher you rank the more bureaucratic your job becomes. Dewey has fond memories of the boots-on-the-ground assignments he has obtained. Once he camped in Death Valley for three months, working on his history of the Scotty's Castle site. I asked Dewey if he has any advice for others. "Don't be afraid to knock on doors," he says. It's how he got started, and he still has to do it all the time when working on his books and oral histories. Dewey has fine people skills but I get the impression that making cold calls is a little daunting for him, as it is for a lot of people.

I asked Dewey about any teaching or mentoring he has done. He informally visits local schools with oral history lessons and lessons on maps. He also leads oral history workshops and walking tours of Point Reyes Station. He does not yet have a protégé to work with as Jack Mason once worked with him, but that may come.

Today the Jack Mason Museum of West Marin History is run by an all-volunteer committee of a 501(c)(3) organization (the Inverness Foundation) which meets monthly. It is housed in "The Gables," a historic building owned by the Inverness Foundation. A detached cottage in the back contains the collection room/archive which includes photographs, large format negatives, original maps dating back to 1871, newspapers, letters, ledgers, portraits, and other artifacts. The museum is open to the public during regular library hours. There is a newsletter, a website, and temporary exhibitions. Members pay dues. Donations, book sales, copying fees, and special events supplement the organization's budget. You can make an appointment to study the archives and you can order copies of historical documents. The museum gratefully accepts donations of money and artifacts. Some other historical societies in our area are run differently: some have a paid director or even a paid staff. Some do not have their own building but occupy a corner of a city hall, library, or school; some are financially broke. The Jack Mason Museum is doing fine. Dewey has contributed a lot of free labor to it over the years, but he has been rewarded personally and professionally. Museum work allowed Dewey to convert his hobby into his career.

• •

A wildlife project

The northern elephant seal (*Mirounga angustirostris*) has an extreme lifestyle. As pups, they nurse on milk that is 50 percent fat, gaining seven or eight pounds per day! But the nursing ends after just a month when the mothers abandon their pups on the beach forever. The pups, who are only four or five weeks old, must teach themselves to swim, find food, and avoid

A bull Northern Elephant Seal (*Mirounga angustirostris*).
Photo by Miles Lim.

sharks. Mortality rates are understandably high. Elephant seals spend most of their lives at sea, diving thousands of feet down in the open ocean for fish and squid, and then coming up for air. They do this continually for months at a time, and our local seals make two trips each year between Northern California and the northeast Pacific, the Aleutian Islands, Hawaii, or even the waters off Russia. They swim over 10,000 miles a year.

When they return to give birth and mate, that's extreme as well. Bulls eighteen feet long and weighing more than your car fight each other brutally on the beach. Males and females fast during their months on the beach and lose hundreds of pounds. Some winter days at the Point Reyes National Seashore there are a thousand seals crowded onto a narrow strip of sand doing all of life's stages at once: fighting, having sex, giving birth, nursing, even dying. It's very loud; almost overwhelming. The seal colonies down the coast from ours are even bigger.

A friend at a social event introduced me to Dr. Sarah Allen, who studies elephant seals. She is a wildlife biologist for the Park Service. She said she wanted high school student volunteers to read tags on elephant seals and do seal censuses, and I didn't have to be asked twice. Now during the fall and winter I and a few trusted students crouch on a bluff overlooking the beach with telescopes, reading the one-inch-long plastic tags that have been attached to the flippers of some of the seals. My daughter participates too; she started in the sixth grade. These tags are like license plates on cars. The color tells where the seal was born: pink for Point Reyes, green for Año Nuevo, white for Piedras Blancas, yellow for San Miguel Island, blue for Mexico, etc. The number is unique to that seal. We record the colors and numbers and also do a census of the seals by sex and age. This isn't easy, because the seals don't always stay still and they laze very close together on the beach.

We give the data to the park service, but we also keep it ourselves and we are starting to notice some intriguing things. There is more variety in the colors of the tags we see on young seals than on breeding females. This must mean that young seals try out different beaches while they are growing up, but once they become pregnant they prefer to go back to the beach where they were born. (Breeding males rarely have tags because they are ten years old or more and the tags have come off.) We are also interested in the question of whether pups born together on the same beach travel together once they leave it (wouldn't you?), and whether elephant seals are shifting northwards up the coast as the climate warms. It looks like they are. When we started, our colony was the northernmost one; it isn't now.

This is really fun. Some people pay to watch elephant seals, but we get front-row seats for free. The students learn a lot from doing it. Even if we never publish anything but student science fair posters, our data is getting added to the Park Service's database, so it is saved for posterity. To make sense of our data my students are starting to correspond with elephant seal researchers to the south of us at the University of California at Santa Cruz and the United States Geological Survey. Thank you, Dr. Allen! Most places don't have elephant seals but wildlife is everywhere, and so are researchers who need help collecting data.

How extreme are elephant seals' lifestyles? My ninth grade daughter wrote this skit for a presentation on her community service hours, which were spent reading flipper tags:

. . . .

THE LIFE OF THE NORTHERN ELEPHANT SEAL—A Short Play by Elise Wing

Cast of Characters:

Cow #1

Cow #2

Bull #1

Bull #2

Pup

Superweaner Pup

COW #1 (Goes up to COW #2 who is snuggling with PUP): Hi girl, I haven't seen you since this time last year! How are you?

COW #2: Oh, you know. Fine—but rearing a pup is hard work when you haven't eaten for a couple of months.

COW #1: I know, right? Fasting while on the beach is a drag.

COW #2: Not to mention having to nurse them all this time . . . Still, there's no experience like having a pup. And you? How are you?

COW #1: Pregnant. Like always.

COW #2: That's right. Get pregnant during the breeding season on the beach, go out to sea for most of the year, swim out to sea alone, dive for squid and seafood, come back to shore, have a pup, get pregnant again. I'm pregnant eleven months of the year!

COW #1: Oh, look—here comes a bull. Let's see what he wants.

BULL #1: Hey, do you want to join my harem?

COW #1: Well . . . How big is your harem?

BULL #1: Just about twenty-five or so.

COW #1: Wow, that's big! And can I hear you trumpet?

BULL #1: (trumpets)

COW #1: You know, you're pretty impressive. I think I might join your harem.

BULL #2: (Comes up to BULL #1): Hey! Is that my wife you're talking to?

BULL #1: She's not yours anymore.

BULL #2: Says who?

BULL #1: Says me!

COW #1: I just want whoever's alpha.

BULL #2: Then let's fight! (Bulls bump chests, make loud noises, grunt, etc. Eventually Bull #2 wins.)

BULL #2: Take that! She's mine now!

COW #2 (to her PUP): Sorry, baby, but I have to go now. I've been nursing you nonstop since you were born and I haven't eaten all this time. I've lost three hundred pounds. I have to go out to sea to find food.

PUP: What? Mommy, I'm only one month old! How can you do this?

COW #2: It's okay. You'll teach yourself to swim and catch food. It's what I did. It's what all elephant seals do. The 50 percent that survive their first year, anyway.

PUP: Whaaaat? (COW #2 leaves)

PUP: NOOOOOO Mommy!

SUPERWEANER PUP: Ha! You must wish you were me.

PUP: Who are you anyway? You're as fat as you are long.

SUPERWEANER PUP: I'm a superweaner! That means after I'd been weaned I found another cow; one whose pup had died; and I nursed from her. I'm practically a sphere of blubbery cuteness! Being a superweaner is awesome because you have less of a chance of starving to death before you learn to catch fish.

PUP: That's a good idea. Maybe I should try it . . . .

THE END

. . . .

A trash project

Everyone likes beachcombing, but local trash isn't as exciting as something that washed up on the beach from a far away place. The great beach at the Point Reyes National Seashore is not like other beaches. This ten-mile stretch of sand faces northwest, into the California current and the prevailing westerly winds. Rocky points bracket it at each end. Most of the manufactured items that wash up here are not local. Some are from thousands of miles away. Every object tells a story.

Our school got a grant from the National Oceanic and Atmospheric Administration's Ocean Guardian Schools program to patrol Point Reyes beaches collecting, counting, weighing, and photographing plastic debris.

Description	Number of items or bags	Total weight in pounds	Brands, Marks and Languages
5-gallon motor oil bucket; oil bottle	2	11	Chevron
crab pot buoys + rope	45	117	
large foam pieces	16	28	
bags of foam pieces	9	13	
bags of plastic water bottles	8	19	Crystal Geyser, Gatorade
bags of misc. plastic	4	24	Lays, Cheetos, Kraft
bags of aluminum cans	3	4.7	Coke, Coors
bags of glass bottles	6	77	Budweiser, Seagrams
bags of crab bait boxes	2	10	
bag of cleaning bottles	1	1.6	Clorox, Dawn
bags of shoes and hats	2	20	Stride Rite
bags of wood, paper, misc. trash	4	22	
large net floats	7	33	Chinese, Japanese
automobile tires	2	55	
bow of small boat/ boat parts	3	59	CF 2589 HW
misc. plastic pieces	42	85	Rubbermaid
tools, plastic buckets	6	2.9	Durabeam
steel propane bottles/ scrap metal	3	4.5	Coleman
political sign	1	0.2	Sally Lieber for Senate
plastic bottle caps	hundreds	4	Coke, Minute Maid
light bulbs	7	1.5	General Electric
metal spray cans	4	2	
mylar balloons	31	1	

Table 1. Debris collected on Point Reyes Beach, Winter 2014

Description	Number of items or bags	Total weight in pounds	Brands, Marks and Languages
plastic toys	44	2.2	Mattel
pens	16	0.1	Bic
oyster farming spacers	45	1	
chewing tobacco tins	14	0.5	Copenhagen
shotgun shell casings	177	1	
balls; mostly tennis balls	25	3	Penn
spoons and forks	15	0.2	
drinking straws	113	0.2	
medicinal, dental, personal care	45	1.3	Cortizone
tampon applicators	8	0.1	
cigarette lighters	21	0.6	Bic
small net floats	14	1.5	
sport fishing gear	23	7.8	
duck decoy	1	1	
water bottles from Asia	26	2	China, Japan, India, Malaysia
TOTAL WEIGHT		617.9	

Table 1 (cont). Debris collected on Point Reyes Beach, Winter 2014

We also measure the length of the largest open-ocean barnacle on each item, as a way of estimating how many months it has been afloat. Plastic debris has writing molded onto it. This lets us categorize it according to its type and probable origin: local beach users, commercial fishermen, from international shipping, from Japan, etc. We compare our results to online data previously obtained on California Coastal Cleanup Day.

We find fishing and crabbing gear from Japan, China, Oregon, and Northern California. There are beverage bottles and food containers labeled for domestic consumption in China, Japan, Korea, India, and Mexico. Many don't have barnacles growing on them, which indicates that they were probably tossed overboard from ships near our coast. There are ballpoint pens with the names and logos of local businesses, shotgun shells, duck decoys, doll's heads, and even political signs. There are large glass light bulbs from ships. There is the usual assortment of food wrappers, children's shoes, and sand toys that you find on any beach.

Some items are just baffling. We found a small plastic cap with "Bay View Federal Savings 1911–1961" printed on it. It is the right size and shape to cap a container for a roll of coins, but a few minutes on the internet shows that Bay View ceased to do business under that name in 1981. Has the cap been sitting on the beach since the 1970s? It looks a little faded, but the plastic is still flexible. It really doesn't look like it has been there that long. And how did it get there?

Besides raising awareness of our global solid waste problem and how North America and Asia are connected by winds, currents, and international trade, the project has become interesting as a result of the 2011 tsunami in Japan. Predictions were made of massive amounts of tsunami debris washing up on America's West Coast. Despite a few early arrivals, that hasn't happened. However, while we pick up fishing floats, polypropylene rope, and plastic water bottles, we keep our eyes out for something related to the tsunami. We know some of it is still out there, somewhere.

Not every school is located so close to a beach like this, but trash is everywhere. Ever since William Rathje found 25-year-old guacamole in a landfill that was still green, garbology has been a recognized field. It can be disturbing and interesting at the same time. It can get addictive if you know where to look for the good stuff.

. . . .

Profiles: Richard Lang and Judith Selby Lang, artists

How do you move your trash project to the next level? I met this husband-and-wife team when they came to talk to my students about the plastic debris on Point Reyes Beach. Their experience in this area is much deeper than mine. For over fifteen years they have made regular patrols of the same 1000-yard stretch of the beach picking up what they find, taking it home, cleaning it, and using it to make art that is thought provoking and visually stunning.

It began when Richard's son had to do community service for school. They went to Kehoe Beach (a section of the great beach at Point Reyes) and picked up some trash. Instead of throwing it away, they took it home. Richard had experience making art with found material. He was educated at the Corcoran College of Art and Design in Washington, D.C., and George

One of Richard and Judith Selby Lang's art pieces using marine plastic debris. Photo by Richard and Judith Selby Lang.

Washington University and holds a Master of Fine Arts (MFA) degree from the University of Wisconsin. In graduate school he did his thesis project in sculpture using scraps left over from other student's projects. After that he worked in two dimensions, painting and making prints, in part because it uses less material than sculpture. Maybe finding the plastic on Kehoe Beach reawakened something in him.

A few years later Judith was visiting Richard's business in San Francisco and noticed an object from the beach on his table. Neither of them knew it yet, but each had been collecting beach plastic. Judith is trained in art also, at Pitzer College, the California Institute of the Arts, and San Francisco State University. She teaches art classes at convalescent hospitals and senior centers through Santa Rosa Junior College's Community Education and

Seniors Program. Her life's work has been teaching art for the elderly and Alzheimer's patients, beginning years ago at the Napa State Hospital. She admired Richard's photos of Kehoe Beach, and they went there on their first date. They got married and have been collaborating ever since. When they spoke to my students, they each talked half of the time and sometimes they finished each other's thoughts.

The Langs do not earn their living making art out of beach plastic. Besides Judith's teaching job they own a small business, called Electric Works, in San Francisco's South-of-Market Street neighborhood. Electric Works makes professional prints for other artists, so they have the best large-format digital equipment there is for scanning, photography, and printmaking, and a big reflection-free studio. This equipment helps the Langs make their plastic debris look good. Electric Works also serves the San Francisco art community as a bookstore and sometimes as a gallery. The Langs are well connected in the art world. I think they built up their network of connections one print job at a time.

After their weekly trips to Kehoe Beach they bring their haul home and wash and dry it. First they sort it by color. The Langs love color. After that, they sort it by category. They store it in bins, boxes, and drawers in a barn on their property. Usually they don't use it to make sculptures. They arrange pieces of plastic on a white background or a ceramic plate, treating each little bit of plastic as an artist's brush stroke. Since they work together, there is a lot of trial-and-error, negotiation, and debate during this process. Once it is arranged to their satisfaction, they make a high-quality digital image of it using their professional equipment. The art they produce is a print of that image. The pieces of plastic go back into their storage bins.

Some of their work is monochromatic. For example, they made a print of a pale yellow Fiestaware plate with an assortment of pale yellow plastic objects on it, including a lemon-shaped juice bottle, a loop for blowing soap bubbles, a hair curler, a party popper, what looks like a swizzle stick, part of a sand toy, leaves from an artificial flower, and some hard-to-identify bits and pieces. All have been bleached by the sun to become the same color as the plate. The effect is pleasing, even beautiful. It looks abstract at first glance or from a distance, but up close you realize how specific and familiar these objects are. More often, they use a rainbow palette. An example from their Cavallo Point series of prints shows a heap of several dozen colorful plastic rings, the kind that surround the mouths of milk bottles to hold the cap in place. They are bright orange, yellow, red, lime green, dark green, pink, and blue. A blue plastic toy shovel lies underneath the pile, ready to scoop up a measure of them, as if they were a useful commodity.

The Langs like to arrange similar found objects in rows and columns as if they were butterflies in a museum drawer. This calls attention to their subtle differences. They have fun with the red plastic cheese spreaders in Kraft Handi-Snacks. When you set these out in a grid, you see they are not all alike. Some have been on the beach longer and are bleached by the sun and eroded by the sand. Some have visible scratches or have been bent, broken, stained, or are missing corners. The Langs wrote letters to Kraft Foods describing how many of these little plastic spreaders they had found on the beach and suggesting some biodegradable alternatives like bamboo. Kraft wrote letters back to them that stressed Kraft's commitment to corporate responsibility and green practices but offered no specific commitment to change their product. A while after that the Langs found a plastic cheese spreader on the beach that was not red, but bright green! They wrote another letter to Kraft saying this is not what they meant by "green" packaging. This time Kraft did not reply. The Langs never did find out the story behind the green cheese spreader, but they showed it to me. Other than the color, it looks exactly like the red ones.

Richard and Judith also find plastic toy soldiers of the type that are olive green and a little over an inch high. Using their high tech equipment, they have magnified the faces of the soldiers and made large individual portraits of them. You might think that all the soldier's faces would look the same, but you would be wrong. Because of differences in the way they were molded and also because of their individual experiences being rolled back and forth in the surf, they are all different. Their faces look ghostly; anguished, slightly incomplete, but human.

When I first met Judith she was wearing a necklace made of large colorful beads. I assumed it was "real" jewelry but on closer inspection it turned out to be Superballs, all found on the beach. The Langs always have great stories to tell about the stuff they find. They told us a story about how the Wham-O company once made a Superball the size of a bowling ball and dropped it off a skyscraper as a promotional stunt. It bounced well. On its second bounce it totaled a parked car. These artists must make great dinner guests.

The Langs have had over forty exhibitions of their work in museums, galleries, and libraries, both locally and overseas. They like non-traditional art venues. They are particularly proud of the year in which they designed the California Coastal Cleanup Day's promotional posters. "Art on the back of the bus!" they say, with awe in their voices.

At the time of this writing they had several exhibits around the San Francisco Bay Area and one in Alaska. I took my children to the Oakland Museum of California. The lowest floor has exhibits on California's natural history. The second floor is for California human history and culture, and the third floor shows California's fine art. Judith and Richard's work could belong on any one of these floors, but you will find it on the natural history floor on permanent display. The art installation "The Great Conveyor" consists of plastic water bottles and blue bottle caps embedded in sheets of clear plastic hung from the ceiling. You stand under it and look up, and it looks like you are underwater viewing the sea's choppy surface from underneath. The bottles and bottle caps look like they are floating in the waves. They look clean, blue, and beautiful. Below is a large countertop with colored pencils and crayons, worksheets for children, and binders of stories and pictures of plastic things the Langs have found. There are also two museum drawers, one containing a rainbow of plastic items and the other an assortment of plastic water bottles packaged for consumption in a variety of countries from Asia and North America. On the countertop are six large apothecary jars filled with plastic: one each for combs, drinking straws, toys, spoons and forks, toothbrushes and cigarette lighters. Everything was found on Kehoe Beach. There is a small library of books on marine plastic debris and a beanbag chair to sit in while you read them. There is a stuffed dead albatross, his belly slit open to show the cupful of plastic debris he ate before he died. A grant from the National Oceanic and Atmospheric Administration (NOAA) paid for this work.

Sausalito's Marine Mammal Center is our region's hospital and veterinary clinic for sick and injured seals. Harbor seals, elephant seals, California sea lions, sea otters, and dolphins that are found in distress are captured and taken to the Center for feeding and medical care. Once they are rehabilitated they are released back into the Pacific Ocean. The public can visit, so my children and I went there too. The Langs have constructed an art exhibit called "The Ghost Below" with two large installations in the Center's courtyard. The name refers to ghost nets, commercial fishing nets made of nylon, polyester, and polypropylene that get loose from fishing vessels and drift for years in the ocean, entangling sea life, before eventually washing up somewhere.

One piece, "The Ghost Net Monster" is a hooded figure about twice the height of a human, made of heaps of plastic fishing nets stretched over a metal frame. Mature viewers might find it campy, but children are sometimes frightened by it. The 450 pounds of netting it is made of were found in the belly of a dead sperm whale that washed up on a beach here. He must have thought it tasted good because of all the entangled sea life it carried, but once he swallowed it he couldn't digest it or spit it up. So, although the art piece is whimsical, the story behind it is sad.

Their other piece at the Marine Mammal Center, "Indra's Net," includes a 40-foot abandoned trawl net stretched out overhead in the courtyard. The Langs purchased the net from another Point Reyes beachcomber, Richard James. Indra, a Hindu deity, is said to have spread an infinite net across the universe. He attached a glittering jewel to each knot in the net so that every jewel sparkles with reflected light from every other jewel. The Lang's net has "jewels" made of plastic bottle caps inset with pieces of mirror. Planet Earth is supported high in the air by one section of the net. Long blue kelp-like streamers hang down to face level from the net, and each "leaf" on the streamers has a handwritten promise from a visitor to be more aware and to take some action to preserve the ocean from pollution. According to the Langs, "The net expresses the interdependence of all life. We are part of those jewels, and our every action reflects on the actions of all others. Our actions—big or small—together make a difference in the health of our oceans." The Marine Mammal Center reached out to the Langs after it had a successful show from an artist in Oregon who also works with beach debris. Specifically, the administrators of the center wanted something done with the net the whale had swallowed. Money from the Pacific Gas & Electric Company paid for the Lang's work at the center.

At the same time as the Oakland Museum and Marine Mammal Center exhibits, the Langs were showing their work at the California Academy of Sciences exhibit "Built for Speed," which coincided with San Francisco's hosting the America's Cup sailboat races. "Built for Speed" included fast-swimming fish, an Oracle Team USA sailboat, an orca skeleton being assembled in front of the visiting public, and environmental exhibits, including plastic stuff from the Lang's collection. Maybe you could call the Lang's contribution to it "built to float slowly." The Langs were invited to do this work because of their reputation. They have a presence on the internet with a number of blogs, websites, YouTube videos, and articles written about them. Even so, they had to submit a competitive proposal and work closely with Academy scientists once they received the approval. Money from Oracle and other donors paid for the work.

Do Judith and Richard have a love affair with plastic? They won't deny the pleasure they get from finding a trophy item while beachcombing. A lot of their work highlights the beauty of plastic items, not the ugliness. Plastic is the medium they are committed to. "Plastic is forever," they say. It's the material of our times, and it's our legacy. They have produced a tongue-in-cheek print like a postcard of a cliff at Kehoe Beach with a layer of plastic debris photoshopped into it partway up the cliff face called the "Plasticene Discontinuity." This is not hyperbole. If fossil trilobites, creatures similar to crabs, can be preserved in rocks from the Cambrian period, then surely our throwaway plastic items will persist in the geologic record for billions of years. A toothbrush is more durable than crab shell.

I asked the Langs about their future plans. This led to a digression about science, Sputnik, logic, intuition, serendipity, "isms," art school, and Judith's being in the seventeenth year of a twenty-five year project. The Lang's don't really know where they are headed, except that they have an ongoing commitment to their 1000-yard stretch of beach.

The Langs don't throw away the stuff they find. They curate it in their barn. They tell their adult children, "someday all this will be yours!" The Langs believe that humor is a better way to get people to change their ways than sanctimony. "Jokes are profound," they say. "Jokes are the key to real intelligence." Judith and Richard told my students that, despite conventional wisdom, it is possible to earn your living in the art world. They have done it for decades, first by themselves and then together. "It's really hard," they warn, but they are smiling broadly as they say it. They told me: "This is the most fun we've ever had in this life."

"Serendipity" is a word the Langs use a lot. In fact, nearly all of the people I have interviewed for this book have invoked it in one way or another. Richard told me, "Our gods are the three princes of Serendip," referring to an oriental fairy tale. The word is nuanced but today it implies luck, chance, and surprise, as well as the wisdom to respond to the unexpected. It's when you know you are looking for something but you don't yet know what it is. "You see things out of the corner of your eye, you hear something or you mishear something, and your imagination takes off from there," Richard says. Judith says, "We say it's serendipity but when we're offered opportunities, we really follow up."

Natural experiments and free data

For a few years I worked in the environmental consulting business, at sites with contaminated soil and groundwater. If you own an industrial site in California where the soil and groundwater have been polluted with hazardous chemicals, the law says you have to clean it up. This can be complicated and expensive, in part because most of these sites have had multiple owners and multiple tenants, were contaminated over periods of many decades, and can have lots of different chemicals from different sources mixed together underground: hydrocarbon fuels, chlorinated solvents, and heavy metals. The work I did was mostly reading reports and writing other reports for clients; that's why I didn't stick with it. I found it boring. One day, though, I heard about a very interesting situation.

A factory had a one-time spill of a chemical called 1,1,1-trichloroethane. That may sound like a jawbreaker of a name to you but any chemist can tell you that this molecule has only eight atoms in it. What was different about this incident was that the soil and groundwater at this location were otherwise clean. The spill was from leaky pipe. It happened and was detected, repaired, and documented all in the same day. However, several dozen gallons of this chlorinated solvent were now in the ground and could not easily be recovered.

Over the years after that, other environmental consultants had drilled wells near the spill and had periodically sampled the groundwater and analyzed it for hazardous chemicals. They had to report it to the State of California. All of this data was available to the public, in the office of the California Regional Water Quality Control Board. Anyone who cared to could walk in and ask to examine the data. It was in big three-ring binders on a bookshelf.

I was probably the only person who ever did that for this site, and I did it for a particular reason: Experts in this field were undecided on how long it takes 1,1,1-trichloroethane to break down into other chemicals underground. Some laboratory experiments had been done, but here was what scientists call a "natural experiment." You can't actually pollute the soil with toxic chemicals in a real place to see what will happen, but somebody had done it accidentally and the data was free for the asking.

I found that the 1,1,1-trichloroethane on this site had decomposed with a half-life of 2.9 years. Every 2.9 years half of it had broken down into other chemicals that we could still detect. That number was higher than what the laboratory studies suggested. I also found that by making a graph over time of the ratio of the decomposition products of 1,1,1-trichloroethane to the amount of it that was still there, I was able to "conclude" from the graph that the spill had happened within one week of when it actually did happen! This has obvious implications for anyone trying to figure out on whose watch a spill happened. Remember, most of these industrial sites have had multiple owners and multiple tenants.

A "natural experiment" is any situation in which the experimental work has already been done, by Mother Nature or by the unintended consequences of human activities. Nobody planned it to obtain data to answer your question, but the data is there and ripe for the picking. You can use it to answer your question. Nobody has looked at it in that way yet. The actual work of collecting the data has already been done by others. There are places you can get lots of data just by asking for it, like the California Regional Water Quality Control Board. In the digital world, data is accumulating faster than anyone can make meaning of it. Find some and use it. I did it in the pre-internet era, and published an original scientific paper for which I didn't have to make any measurements or spend one dime on chemical analyses: Wing M.R. (1997) "Apparent first-order kinetics in the transformation of 1,1,1-trichloroethane in groundwater following a transient release." *Chemosphere*. Volume 34, Number 4, pages 771–781.

"I Dwell in Possibility"

The experiences I've described in this chapter, particularly meeting Dewey Livingston and the Langs, made me explore the limits of what is possible and what isn't for a person with only ordinary access to resources. Most people spend their lives doing the things that others expect of them, and not much more. For instance a K-12 teacher like me might simply teach his classes and then go home, as I had done for years.

I started to look for the exceptions—people who had accomplished unusual things—in the natural sciences, social sciences, and the arts, despite not having a university appointment, a powerful job, great personal wealth, or even genius. I found some. They had things in common. They started small, then sought affiliations and collaborations. They applied for things, often compulsively. They traveled with a sense of mission; not just for fun. They published their work, and taught others. Most of all, they seemed happier than the rest of us. Their activities added structure and purpose to their daily lives and their accomplishments were very satisfying. I became convinced that most of us have unrealized potential. The chapters that follow offer techniques I've learned from them for realizing that potential.

2

Have Affiliations and Collaborate

"A whale ship was my Yale College and my Harvard."
—Herman Melville, *Moby Dick*

It really helps to be able to represent yourself as more than just your-self. Affiliation gives you access to resources, opens doors, confers status, and gives you credibility in your dealings with others. A college or univer-sity affiliation is a valuable asset because universities have libraries and collections and helpful librarians and you may need to do some library or collections research to pursue your project. You don't need to be a full-time student or staffer to get a university library card. Schools, government agencies, museums and libraries, technology companies, historical soci-eties, arts organizations, TV or radio stations, newspapers, and environ-mental organizations are also possible affiliates. If you work for one of the organizations listed above you already have an affiliation. If you don't there are a lot of titles you can negotiate with one of them that include the words "adjunct," "visiting," "associate," "volunteer," "in residence," "researcher," "docent," "intern," or "board member" singularly or in combination.

As an example, let's look at the Point Reyes National Seashore, a medium-sized park near my home. The seashore has beaches, tide pools, a light-house, historic ranches, Morgan horses, mature forests, whales, seals, elk, and many species of birds. A little over one hundred people work there. Besides the superintendent, there are trails and maintenance workers, carpenters, interpretive specialists, ecologists and wildlife biologists, fish-eries experts, hydrologists, water quality technicians, rangers, dispatchers, firefighters, a historian, an archaeologist, a museum curator, and an archi-vist. There are also seasonal employees and volunteer docents.

Anyone can become an elephant seal docent, a harbor seal docent, a snowy plover docent, or an elk docent. These positions involve being outdoors in the field in certain seasons, monitoring the animals, protecting them from visitors, and educating the visitors about the animals. Volunteers also care for the park's retired Morgan horses. The park's Pacific Coast Science and Learning Center, a field station, has dozens of interns (paid and unpaid) working on specialized ecology projects. The Cordell Bank National Marine Sanctuary is headquartered at the park, and it has its own programs. The Point Reyes National Seashore Association Field Institute teaches classes on natural history, outdoor recreation, and art. While not strictly a part of the park, Point Blue Conservation Science (formerly the Point Reyes Bird Observatory) has dozens of ways to get involved in bird and ecosystem research. It is easy to get involved in a project or start a project at Point Reyes.

That's one park. The San Francisco Bay Area has several other national parks and monuments and a number of state parks. It also has Stanford University, the Universities of California at Berkeley and San Francisco, San Francisco State and Sonoma State Universities, the Lawrence Berkeley and Lawrence Livermore National Laboratories, the NASA Ames Research Center, the U. S. Geological Survey, the California Academy of Sciences, the Lawrence Hall of Science, the de Young Museum, the Palace of the Legion of Honor, the Asian Art Museum, the Tech Museum of Innovation, the Oakland Museum of California, the San Francisco Public Library, the San Francisco Museum and Historical Society, the San Francisco Symphony, the San Francisco Opera, the U. S. Army Corps of Engineers' San Francisco Bay Model, the California Coastal Commission, the California Native Plants Society, the Sierra Club, and the technology companies in Silicon Valley: Google, Facebook, Apple, Hewlett-Packard, etc. All of these institutions offer ways to become affiliated.

Depending on where you live, your list of scientific and cultural institutions may be shorter, but the chances are good that several organizations that are right for you are located within an hour's drive of where you live. Read their websites, talk to people, and explore your options. As a full time teacher, my primary affiliation is with my school, Sir Francis Drake High School. I also have arrangements (with varying degrees of formality) with NASA, the National Park Service, the University of California, and the Mars Institute.

One easy way to get a collaboration started is to approach a university professor. For example, sometimes school teachers do scientific research in a university professor's lab over the summer. There are formal programs that match teachers with professors and often pay the teacher a stipend. In my area, the IISME (Industry Initiatives for Science and Math Education) Summer Fellowship Program places teachers in labs at technology companies and universities. The stipend is $8,200 for eight weeks. Sometimes people who are not university students or teachers visit a professor's office anyway, explain their backgrounds, pitch their services, and make their own informal arrangements. Sometimes the professor and the outside person know each other already, professionally or socially. The professor gets a motivated and (presumably) capable person to join his or her research group for free. Sometimes the informal arrangement leads to a more formal one later, involving a job title, pay, or enrollment in a graduate program.

Affiliation with any of the types of organizations listed above implies some sort of collaboration with a person there. It's a rare institution that you can join without talking to people. You will want to do that, because your best opportunities and ideas are going to arise from chance interactions with others. The technology company Yahoo! got a lot of media attention when it banned working from home for most of its employees. Yahoo!'s rationale wasn't that people who work alone aren't productive. They are very productive. It was that they are not innovative enough to pull their weight in a technology company.

Profile: Richard V. Wing, classicist

One of the most scholarly people anywhere is my father, Richard Wing. He has three advanced degrees. He went to law school twice, for fun. He has never practiced law, except a few times as favors to friends, and he never intended to. As he neared retirement, he began to study classical civilizations and became an authority on the coins of ancient Greece.

Richard earned a B.S. in engineering and applied physics at Harvard and worked full time for over thirty years at a technology company, Honeywell, eventually leading a department. During these years he was also a family man, raising three children, serving as a scoutmaster, collecting coins, and sailing on Cape Cod. Whenever he wasn't doing those things, he was studying, usually law but sometimes business or classical art and archaeology. None of his advanced degrees earned income for him; all the money he made was from his engineering career.

He says his legal journey began when we lived in San Diego for a few years and he had an early morning commute on Interstate 5 north of downtown. The University of San Diego's campus is on a hill overlooking the I-5 valley, and its towers and domes would glow in the morning sun even while the valley was still dark. It is still a beautiful sight today, and perhaps it made Richard homesick for Harvard. He started taking night classes at the law school and when we moved back to Boston he transferred to Suffolk University. Honeywell paid for his tuition at both schools and even paid for the bar exam cram course. In those days it was common for large companies to invest in their employees this way.

He liked law school. He would laugh with pleasure during some of the exams he took, because he often anticipated in advance the questions the professors would ask. Suffolk told him they wouldn't use his first year grades in calculating his class rank, because they were from a different school. His first year grades hadn't been great, but in his second year he flourished as a student and when he received his Doctor of Jurisprudence degree (J.D.), he was in the top 1 percent of his class. Needless to say, he passed the bar exam.

The J.D. is the only degree a person needs to become anything in the legal profession: an attorney, a judge, even a law professor. Richard had such a good time in law school that he went back for more, enrolling in night classes at Boston University to study for a L.L.M. (Master of Legal Letters) degree. He wrote his master's thesis on whether computer software counts as a "tangible asset" for property tax purposes. "That was a mistake," he laughed. Several years into his second law program, he came to realize what most of us already know: Tax law is hard and boring. However, Honeywell was still paying his expenses and he was nearly done, so he finished the requirements for the degree.

Richard was laid off by Honeywell during an economic downturn. Middle-aged and in a recession, he knew it would be hard to get another technology job. He had a pension from Honeywell and some savings, and his wife had a good job. He knew he had enough money but he needed a project to work on. He had already started taking night classes in ancient Greek. (Boston University allows any person who is 58 or older to audit almost any class, space permitting, and there is always going to be space in the ancient Greek classes.) He went to Harvard University's extension school to study classical civilizations. The extension school is taught by real Harvard professors, often very senior ones. Richard came to know

Professor David Mitten, the curator of ancient art. After he took a few classes, Professor Mitten told him, "It's time for you to go to Greece" and arranged for him to go to the American School of Classical Studies in Athens for the summer.

Back at Harvard, Richard continued taking classes. One day he was standing in the ancient coin room with Professor Mitten. A wealthy collector, a Mr. H. Bartlett Wells, had recently donated to Harvard his collection of over 3,000 ancient coins. Professor Mitten said, "I wish *someone* would catalog the Wells collection." There was a long silence. Nobody else was in the room, so Richard said, "I'll do it." It took him ten years to complete the job. Along the way he earned a Master of Liberal Arts in Extension from Harvard. He was given the title of "Curatorial Assistant," a Harvard ID card, and a campus parking pass.

Cataloging the Wells collection was so much work because each of the 3,000 coins needed to be described, interpreted, photographed, placed in its historical context, and compared to similar coins known from other collections around the world. If a coin is unique, then the only way to find that out is to research the literature from all the world's major ancient coin collections. While cataloging the collection, Richard became the go-to person in the classics department whenever a professor needed a guest lecturer on ancient coins or a substitute teacher, or whenever a visiting scholar needed a tour. He gave lectures and seminars at Harvard and also for the Boston Numismatic Society.

An archaeologist at Brown University, Professor Martha Sharp Joukowsky, invited him to be a member of an expedition to the Greek island of Corfu. "It was pick-and-shovel work in the 109 degree heat," he recalled. But the team found lots of coins for him to identify. "At first we thought we had found a brothel," he says, because there were many coins and lamps in an area next to the public baths. But the denominations of the coins were too high for that. They also found a skeleton, a victim of an earthquake, cut in half by a fallen stone wall. He had a sheath knife strapped to his leg. They named him Spiro. Richard paid for his own airfare on this trip and for most of his food, but Brown provided his lodging and some festive Greek dinners.

Richard also became the president of the Society Historia Numorum, a private club consisting of classics professors, coin dealers, and elite coin collectors from the greater Boston area. They meet each month at some-body's house to enjoy good food and drink and hear lectures on ancient coins. Membership is capped at twenty, so no matter how qualified you are, you can't join until an existing member resigns. As president, his job is to line up the venues and speakers.

Besides the catalog of the Wells collection, Richard's main publications have been photographs of coins in *The Celator*, a magazine for ancient coin enthusiasts. One of his photos has been on the cover of Cornell University's alumni magazine. Richard does not write articles about coins, but he is skilled with a camera and is always happy to take professional photographs of coins for the people who do. Richard has also developed a recent interest in maritime relics. These are coin-like commemorative medals made from metal taken from famous ships.

Although Richard did a little coin collecting for much of his life, he didn't come to know ancient Greek coins until he was near retirement. His expertise in that area was acquired past the age of fifty, and a lot of it wouldn't have happened without his coursework and affiliation with Harvard's extension school. All major universities in urban areas have some kind of extension school or program designed for working adults to take classes in the evenings and on weekends. Some, like the University of California at Berkeley's programs, are strictly about gaining specific job skills in professional fields. Others, like Harvard's, are for the liberal arts and sciences. Some allow you to earn an accredited degree, while others offer professional certificates. The cost of these "extension" courses is usually only a small fraction of the cost of similar courses in the regular degree programs, and there is little competition to get into them. If you have been out of academia for a while, this avenue may be a way to get back into it.

AARP, Inc. (formerly the American Association of Retired Persons) has 40 million members like my father. Not all seniors have scholarly interests or are financially secure but millions of older people, working and retired, fit this description. Three out of four Americans say they intend to do paid work part-time after retiring from their career. They believe they will want to work or they will need the money, or both. Curiously, when the time comes, only 19 percent of them actually work part-time for pay. This disconnect between people's expectations for retirement and what they actually do was the subject of a *New York Times* article titled "The Gray Jobs Enigma." The reasons vary. Some experience poor health, or need to care for a family member with health problems. Some realize that they don't need the money after all. Some can't find suitable part-time work. They face age discrimination or have outdated skills. Whatever the reasons, over half of our older population expects to do paid work after retirement but won't. What will take its place? For some, like Richard Wing, a project will take its place.

. . . .

University Extension Schools

There's something exhilarating about walking across campus at an elite university, scuffling the autumn leaves, admiring the grassy lawns, the big trees, the architecture, noticing the professors and students coming and going, and knowing that you're a part of it, too. For some people, there's no substitute for being on a big, beautiful campus. I am one of those people. I just feel a glow inside. Richard Wing obviously feels that way too. Going back to school is one way to get that prepared mind that chance will favor.

Major universities are more accessible to you than you may think, because most offer part-time and evening extension school programs. The regular full-time degree programs at these institutions are exclusive, expensive, and require a big commitment of time and energy. Extension school programs are generally easy to get into, less expensive, and self-paced. They make it simple to take classes, earn a degree, get a collaboration started, maybe even to teach at the university level.

Harvard University was a pioneer in this area over a century ago, when it partnered with the Lowell Institute, a program of free and low-cost public lectures for citizens of Boston on philosophy, science, and the arts. The Lowell Institute also offered an evening school on the Massachusetts Institute of Technology's campus called the School for Industrial Foremen. This school was eventually transferred to Northeastern University, but meanwhile Harvard expanded the Lowell Institute's other offerings with open enrollment evening courses on campus and degree programs offered to working adults in the Boston area at a modest cost. The classes are usually taught on campus by regular Harvard instructors. There are no admission requirements to take extension courses at Harvard.

The surprising result of this is that if you don't already have a bachelor's degree, you can earn one at Harvard without ever having to deal with the Harvard College admissions office. You don't have to tell them your high school grades or SAT scores or get letters of recommendation, and the cost is a small fraction of the tuition in the daytime program. All you have to do (as of this writing) is to take three extension courses and get a B or better in them. One of them has to be an expository writing course. Then you tell the extension school you want to be admitted into the ALB (Bachelor of Liberal Arts in Extension) program. They admit almost everybody who asks. You can choose from about twenty areas of study, including anthropology, biology, computer science, economics, English, environmental studies, history, math, philosophy, and Spanish. Your degree will say "Bachelor of Liberal Arts in Extension from Harvard University" instead of "Bachelor of Arts from Harvard College." Outside of Cambridge, Massachusetts, most people wouldn't understand this distinction.

Assuming you already have a bachelor's degree, you could have gone to Harvard instead! But you still can, because the extension school also offers an ALM (Master of Liberal Arts in Extension) program. Again, there are about twenty areas of concentration in the liberal arts and sciences and also some specialized programs like biotechnology, information technology, and mathematics for teaching. The graduate courses are more expensive than the undergraduate courses, but they're still a lot cheaper than the tuition in a regular daytime graduate school.

This is a really good deal. The *New York Times* wrote an article about it titled "Harvard, for Less: Extension Courses' New Allure." My father earned his ALM at the extension school and also went to Harvard College and earned a bachelor's degree the traditional way in the 1950s. He says the quality of instruction was equally good in both programs.

The University of Pennsylvania also has programs for part-time and older students. The College of Liberal & Professional Studies' flexible Master of Liberal Arts program has daytime and evening courses. In the Master of Philosophy in Liberal Arts program, you write a master's thesis. This seems a lot like Harvard's ALM program, although it is more expensive. Penn also has professional certificates and degrees, and part-time and nontraditional undergraduate programs. The Johns Hopkins University's Advanced Academic Programs offer graduate degrees, professional certificates, and noncredit programs, all of them flexible and part time, with evening classes. One of these is the Master of Liberal Arts degree, which consists of ten courses taught by regular Johns Hopkins faculty. Georgetown University's School of Continuing Studies has Bachelor of Arts in Liberal Studies, Master of Arts in Liberal Studies (MALS), and Doctor of Liberal Studies degree programs and some professional master's degree and certificate programs.

Northwestern University's School of Continuing Studies has part-time undergraduate and graduate programs with evening and weekend classes in the arts and sciences. So, like Harvard, Penn, and Georgetown, Northwestern offers a pathway to a bachelor's degree that bypasses the office of undergraduate admissions. (Do the millions of stressed-out high school students around the world who want to attend prestigious universities know about this?) Northwestern's Master of Arts in Liberal Studies (MALS) requires nine courses and a master's thesis. The University of Chicago's Graham School of Continuing Liberal and Professional Studies has certificate programs and graduate programs, including their Master of Liberal Arts, Master of Arts in Teaching, and Graduate Student-at-Large programs.

The University of London is not a single institution, but a collection of self-governing schools and institutes, including University College London, King's College, and the London School of Economics. Since 1920, Birkbeck College has been the University of London's night school. Birkbeck goes back further than that, though, starting early in the 19th century as the London Mechanic's Institute. It sounds like it was similar to the Lowell Institute's industrial foremen's school. Birkbeck's earliest meetings were actually held in a tavern! Birkbeck has full-time and part-time bachelors, masters and Ph.D. programs in the arts and sciences, all of them taught in the evenings.

You can see a familiar pattern for the MLA (Master of Liberal Arts) extension school degree: taught at night on the campus of a prestigious university, part-time, resulting in an accredited master's degree at a relatively low cost. Near my home, Stanford University has this option. Although it is not very different from the programs mentioned above, let's take a closer look at the details of what is offered.

Stanford's MLA Program is just one offering in a large galaxy of continuing studies programs at this university. This one is pure interdisciplinary liberal arts: the human condition, including anthropology, psychology, the sciences, geography, economics, and literature. It is a part-time program taught one evening a week on Stanford's campus. It takes four to five years to complete, and is taught by regular Stanford professors. First, you take three foundation courses, and a class called "Introduction to Graduate Study." This class takes you into the Stanford libraries where you are taught how to do modern library research, and the fundamentals of writing, presenting ideas, and leading a seminar. Who among us, no matter what academic accomplishments we already have, would not benefit from this? Seven seminar classes follow, each on specialized topics. Then you write a master's thesis of 75–100 pages under the supervision of the Stanford faculty. Your classmates are a diverse community of excellent scholars, from retired professionals looking for some intellectual stimulation to young strivers hoping to use the MLA as a stepping stone into a Ph.D. program.

The charge for tuition is significantly less than Stanford's daytime master's degree programs. You have four or five years to come up with the money a little at a time. There is a 20 percent discount for teachers or retired teachers, and an even larger discount for Stanford employees. I already have an advanced degree, but I think about doing this program when I am older, like my father before me.

Some major universities only offer professional programs for part-time students studying in the evenings. At these places, you can't study the traditional liberal arts and sciences part-time, at least not at the graduate level, not for a degree, and not in the evenings. Maybe one of their specialized programs appeals to you, however, or maybe, if you have the right experience, you can teach a course in one of these programs.

This has been true for me. During my years in the environmental consulting industry, I took six courses for a professional certificate in environmental management from the University of California at Berkeley's extension school. I never finished the requirements for the certificate, and the program is no longer offered. However, the courses only cost a few hundred dollars each, I learned some professionally useful things, and I made some good contacts. I ended up co-teaching an evening course (with Dr. William Motzer) at the UC Berkeley campus on the geology and geochemistry of hazardous waste.

This happened because Dr. Motzer offered a course through UC Berkeley Extension called Forensic Geochemistry. It covered the use of geochemical concepts in legal proceedings, often involving soil and groundwater contamination by hazardous chemicals. There are techniques you can use to determine where the chemicals came from and how long they have been in the ground. This information can be worth a lot of money in cases where several corporations are debating who is responsible for the cleanup. Plus, it is as interesting and challenging to somebody trained in geochemistry as anything in a Sherlock Holmes story! You can bet I signed up for that course. But it was cancelled because of a lack of enrollment. There weren't enough budding forensic geochemists that year. Chagrined, I wrote a letter to Dr. Motzer inviting myself to talk to him. Later on, when he decided to offer the course on hazardous waste, he called me up and invited me to co-teach it with him. It was in the evenings on the UC Berkeley campus, in the geology building. Most of the students were working professionals, but there were also a few regular daytime UC Berkeley geology students in it, both undergraduates and graduate students. I worked hard to prepare for it. We were only paid a few thousand dollars, and that money had to be split two ways. We didn't get rich, but I was teaching a class at one of the world's most prominent universities. I would have done it for free.

Other universities with large extension programs that are mostly about professional work are Boston University, Columbia University, New York University, the University of California at Los Angeles, and the University of Toronto. Boston University also allows anyone 58 or older to audit almost any course (space permitting) for less than $200 through their Evergreen Program. An appendix at the end of this book lists web addresses for these universities' extension schools and programs.

• •

Profile: William E. Motzer, expert witness

Bill Motzer grew up in New York City and earned his B.S., M.S., and Ph.D. in geology from the University of Idaho. His choice of college seems to have perplexed his mother: He recalls getting on the plane to Idaho while telling her, "That's where the rocks are, Mom." In between earning degrees he did stints in the United States Air Force and as an exploration geologist for mining companies. For his Ph.D. work, he did mineral surveys for the United States Geological Survey in Idaho's Bitterroot Mountains, flying from location to location by helicopter.

In the 1980s he came to California just as a new industry was emerging called environmental consulting. Laws had been passed regulating the storage of fuels and chemicals in underground storage tanks. "All those single-wall steel tanks corroded like heck", he says. "We found contamination all over the place." If you pollute the groundwater in California, you have to clean it up. This is time-consuming and expensive, something the owners of the tanks need help with. Companies of engineers and geologists were forming to do the work. Soon it became evident that Silicon Valley had similar problems with the chlorinated solvents used in manufacturing computer chips. After that, it was dry cleaning establishments. Having gotten into the industry at the beginning, Bill educated himself on each new type of chemical contaminant as it came along. He became an expert on how chemicals like perchlorate, hexavalent chromium, nitrate, and mercury behave underground.

I hadn't seen Bill for a very long time so I invited myself over to his company, Todd Engineers, to talk with him again. Bill has done almost five hundred projects for clients. Not all involve contaminated groundwater; many are about drilling wells for clean groundwater. Every technical report his company has written lines the shelves of a huge wall. They contain millions of data points on the chemistry of groundwater. Bill doesn't have to make chemical measurements himself. He orders groundwater samples to be sent to commercial labs; the clients pay the cost. His job is to understand the results.

Because of his experience and his natural curiosity, Bill is well qualified to write articles to help other groundwater professionals understand this complex and always-changing field. He has written a few book chapters in edited volumes and dozens of articles in journals like *Environmental Forensics* and professional newsletters like the Groundwater Resources Association of California's *Hydrovisions* and the American Chemical Society's *The Vortex*. These have titles like "Fingerprinting Water," "Perchlorate: Problems, Detection, and Solutions," and "The Dirt on Dry Cleaning, Part 4." Some of his articles look into the future and assess "emerging contaminants" like prions, nanomaterials, and platinum group metals. These are substances that hardly anybody thinks about as groundwater pollution, as of yet. There was a time when nobody thought about diesel fuel and chlorinated solvents that way either.

Bill teaches and gives talks at professional meetings. Besides the University of California at Berkeley extension courses mentioned above, he has taught a course for the University of Wisconsin Extension (I took it) and speaks several times a year for organizations like the Geological Society of America, the Northern California Professional Environmental Marketing Association, and the Groundwater Resources Association. He is a past president of the San Francisco Bay Branch of the latter organization, and has led field trips to a historic mercury mine for the Northern California Geological Society.

Publishing papers, giving talks, and teaching courses isn't necessary to do the regular work Bill does most of the time (writing technical reports), but these activities give Bill the credibility to do litigation support. This means consulting for lawyers on environmental cases and serving as an expert witness. Bill testifies under oath a few times a year. Being an expert witness isn't like anything else in law. Everybody else is asked under oath to tell the facts. Only expert witnesses are asked specifically for their professional *opinion*. Bill's opinion is valued, because of his experience, his publications, his Ph.D., and because he is very good at explaining things. "Using real science to explain things, rather than just having people fly off the handle—that's what I love about it," he says. "That's one of the reasons I write articles for *The Vortex*." Expert witnessing is lucrative. Bill's company charges twice his standard hourly rate for time spent testifying.

I asked Bill for his advice to other geologists. "Find some particular niche. Forensic geochemistry has been particularly useful to me. That perchlorate paper and my work on chromium six was part of the reason why Todd hired me. I've been working steadily since 1986." In contrast, geologists who do minerals exploration don't keep their jobs long. "Every time the price of gold dropped below three hundred dollars an ounce, I got laid off! There's this saying that geologists are like mushrooms—they are covered in manure, they are kept in the dark, and they are the first to get canned." I have paraphrased; Bill used some more salty language.

Bill is well past the age when most people retire. He's considering it, but appears to still be having too much fun working to feel any urgency. He values the mental challenges he gets from his job and the extra things he does like the writing, speaking, publishing, and testifying. "What would I do? For me, retirement can't just mean going down to the senior center," he says. He expressed interest about some of the other people profiled in this book, and what they do. I promised to give him a copy. Bill has taken a corporate job that is specialized and highly technical, and maybe even a little dull to describe, and has expanded its potential enormously.

Profile: Raymond "Bones" Bandar, collector

The California Academy of Sciences was having a special exhibit on skulls, so I went with my daughter and her friend. The exhibit hall is a huge space. Near the entrance lurked an African elephant skull, looking like one of Henry Moore's sculptures. Elephant skulls have small and indistinct eye sockets, but they have a really large hole high up on the forehead where the nerves that control the trunk pass through. They look like Cyclops skulls, and in fact, the ancient Greek idea of the Cyclops may have arisen from finding fossil elephant skulls. Along the back wall over 400 skulls of California sea lions are mounted in a giant array. However, a few non-sea lion skulls are mixed in with them to keep the viewer on his or her toes. There's a wolf, a wild pig, a bear, and other skulls that look like sea lions from a distance.

The glass cases of skulls are organized by structural themes: notable jaws, ear structures, multipurpose noses, fish heads, bird bills, teeth, antlers, and horns. Each case demonstrates the wide diversity found within each of these homologous structures. A case devoted to carnivores vs. herbivores shows how the orientation of the eye sockets reflects whether the animal is predator or prey: "Eyes in the front, the animal hunts. Eyes on the side, the animal hides." A case of dog skulls shows the extreme variety of forms to be found in this one species. A case containing a gharial, an Amazon River dolphin, and a longnose gar shows how a reptile, mammal, and fish have evolved similar snouts for a similar purpose. This is called convergent evolution.

There is a sketching table with paper and pencils for artists to try their hand at sketching skulls. My daughter and her friend are both artistic, so they spent a long time at the table. While they were at work, I admired the "oddities/trauma" case: sea lion skulls with buckshot holes or embedded monofilament netting; a mountain lion skull with a bear tooth stuck in the cranium; a mule deer with "cactus" antlers, a mutation which makes him look like a crystal-growing experiment gone wrong; a skull of a Churro, the famous four-horned sheep kept by the Navajo. These sheep have a horn-splitting gene that makes each horn divide into two at the base.

You can imagine how surprised I was to learn that one person collected, cleaned, and prepared most of these skulls and that he isn't even an employee of the Academy. His name is Ray Bandar, and he has been doing this for sixty years. He has collected about 7,000 skulls, including 2,000 skulls of California sea lions. He is a retired high school biology teacher with a background in art. His title at the Academy is "Field Associate," a volunteer position. On the third floor of the Academy, in the library, more of his skulls are on display. These he has curated personally, with hand-written cards pointing out notable features or telling stories about each one. My favorite is a big boxy northern elephant seal skull, California's largest native animal.

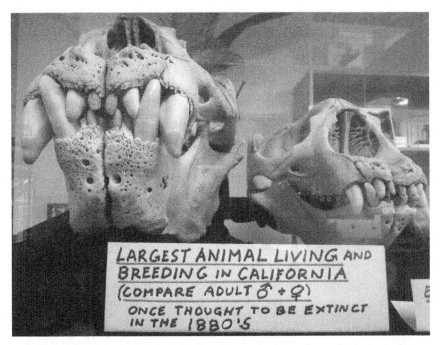

**Two of Ray Bandar's 7,000 skulls. These are of northern elephant seals.
Photo by Michael Wing.**

I asked him for an interview. I had so many questions. How did he get started? Why does he love skulls so much? How did he negotiate his affiliation with the Academy? Where does an urban high school teacher get the head of a giraffe, walrus, warthog, wolf, dachshund, platypus, anteater, etc., anyway? What about federal laws and permits? How does he clean the skulls? Is he squeamish? What does his wife think of all this?

Ray is a fit, enthusiastic octogenarian with an infectious grin and a story for everything. Some of his stories are pretty wild, like the time he damaged his Volkswagen bus trying to pull the head off a dead elephant. His house is full of art and bones. Some people may have skeletons in the closet, but for Ray it's not a metaphor. Ray has skeletons in every room and many more in the basement. There are antlers in the bathtub. For a couple of hours, he graciously took me on a tour of his collections; he knew the origin of every item he showed me. I took twelve pages of notes. Ray is used to this sort of attention; his life's work has been the subject of articles, documentaries, and books. The cartoonist Gary Larson once got the same tour I did; Ray has that same goofy mix of science and humor that's celebrated in Larson's comic *The Far Side.*

Ray grew up in San Francisco and spent almost all his life there. As a child he lived within walking distance of Golden Gate Park, the California Academy of Sciences, and the de Young Museum of Fine Arts. This stimulated his passions for animals and art. Ray used to catch live amphibians and reptiles in the city and offer them to the Steinhart Aquarium; he remembers seeing "donated by Raymond Bandar" labels on the terraria while he was still in junior high school. The staff called him "Reptile Ray." A series of scholarships and the G. I. Bill allowed him to study at art schools from kindergarten through college. Ray graduated from the California College of Arts and Crafts in Oakland where he met his wife Alkmene, who is also an artist. He worked for a few years as a carpenter and then went back to school to earn a biology degree and a teaching credential at San Francisco State University.

He collected his first skull in the 1950s. He was bodysurfing on Ocean Beach and found a dead harbor seal. Something made him fetch a tool, return to the beach, and detach the head from the body. He carried the head home on the bus. It was not particularly fresh. At home he put it in a pot on the kitchen stove to boil off the flesh. The house started to smell. Ray still lived with his parents. Needless to say, his parents weren't amused when they returned home. The next time, Ray buried the skull in the yard.

When Ray married Alkmene, he owned a total of three seal skulls. For their honeymoon, they went on an 11-week road trip across the USA and Canada in her convertible. They camped everywhere, including on the National Mall right below the Washington Monument. In New York they visited the American Museum of Natural History. It was a life-changing moment for Ray: "The gallery of articulated skeletons—seeing the architecture under the skin and muscles—it was so exciting!" In Colorado, Alkmene said, "Stop the car; I see a skeleton." They collected a horse skull, pelvis, and vertebrae. Closer to home, the deserts of Utah and Nevada gave them bones of sheep, cows, and deer. On their return to San Francisco the convertible was piled high with bones.

One day at San Francisco State, a professor told Ray about a job opening at the California Academy of Sciences and directed him to go, right then, for an interview. Ray was dressed in his collector's clothes; he looked like a bum. There was no time to go home and change or get a haircut, which he needed. At the Academy the other two candidates had on suits and ties, but

Ray was offered the job right away. He ran a training program for students. He liked the job, but it paid $2 an hour and wasn't quite full-time. Even then, this was not a lot of money. Once he earned his teaching credential he got a job teaching biology at Fremont High School in east Oakland. So he told the Academy he was resigning. His boss said, "I'm not letting you go—I'm making you a Field Associate." As a high school teacher, Ray had summers off, spring break, and a long winter break. The academy sent him on some of its expeditions during these times. He went to Mexico's cloud forest and to the islands in the Sea of Cortez. He served as the entomologist and herpetologist on these expeditions, but also collected bones. Alkmene would come, too, with her easel and art supplies. In those days every beach in Mexico had bones on it, such as those of whales and sea turtles. Ray and Alkmene made many return trips on their own to Baja California and Sonora.

To get more bones, Ray and Alkmene drove their VW bus to Alaska one summer. They would visit native villages and Ray would ask the children, "Where do you dump the carcasses of the animals you hunt?" This way he picked up skulls from bears, wolves, moose, and caribou. He also visited taxidermy shops in Fairbanks. They returned from Alaska with a busload of great finds. Later they took a trip to Australia to do the same thing. Ray had the proper permits to collect in Australia. A former student who became an entomologist there helped arrange them. (This student named a Mexican species of cricket after Ray: *Inyodectes bandari*. Ray was the first to collect it; his former student described it in the scientific literature.) Despite having his paperwork in order, the customs officials made Ray nervous. Returning from the Australia trip he hung back in the line at the airport watching the different officers at work and trying to decide which one would give him the least hard time. Finally he made his choice:

"What's in these boxes?"

"Would you believe they are full of skulls and bones of animals from Australia?"

"Is anything alive in there?

(Fingers crossed:) "No."

(Some jokes and banter:) "You can go."

Ray had to cross his fingers while saying "no" because he knew there might be live flies, beetles, and maggots in the boxes. He solved the problem by putting the boxes unopened into the Academy's freezer. The invertebrate stowaways were killed. Another time he had to hand-carry a box labeled "IGUANAS" onto an airplane. It really had live rattlesnakes and live fish-eating bats. He took the fish-eating bats into his classroom to show his students.

Zoos, taxidermy shops, and a local tallow works also provided Ray with dead animals. For a time the San Francisco Zoo and the Oakland Zoo would let Ray know when an animal had died. This is where he got most of his skulls from African and Asian animals. The rest of the animal was usually incinerated. The tallow works provided dogs and cats that the Humane Society had euthanized.

Despite these sources of bones, Ray never stopped collecting on beaches. There is a hotline to report dead marine mammals and for many years the messages went to Ray. His territory extended across five northern California counties. Often he would just patrol a beach. Ravens and vultures might lead him to a dead seal. Collecting on beaches is not easy. You walk on sand for miles. You smell like dead seal afterwards. Once he got lost in the rain and slept under a bush overnight. People don't always understand what Ray is up to; sometimes onlookers have objected strenuously to his taking apart a dead animal, even though he is legally authorized to do it. He has been trapped against a cliff by a rising tide. Once he was chased by a bull elephant seal and he slipped and fell. He had the presence of mind to roll sidewise. Ray showed me photos of himself working on a dead sperm whale that washed up on a beach. It had swallowed some netting, and I realized that this was the same net used for a sculpture by Richard and Judith Lang, who are profiled earlier in this book.

Preparing a skull is a messy job. After separating a head from the rest of the carcass, Ray would bring it back to the Academy where for many years he had a lab on the roof. He would remove the brains through the foramen magnum, the hole at the base of the skull. If the animal is at all decomposed, the brains are pretty much liquid and can almost be poured out. Next he would mechanically cut off as much of the skin and flesh as he could. The skeletons and bones of small animals get cleaned up by dermestid ("flesh eating") beetles at the Academy. Larger skulls get placed in buckets of water to soak for a long time. Bacterial action decomposes the remaining soft tissue. Really large bones get buried in soil for a year or more, sometimes on the grounds of the zoo where they lived. Once that's done, the bones are usually bleached, either chemically or by being left in the sun on the Academy's roof. The skulls in the Academy's exhibit don't look like dead animals. They are beautiful, as clean as porcelain.

Most of what Ray has done would be illegal today if you or I tried it. The Marine Mammal Protection Act prohibits the taking of seal parts. You can't collect anything, not even seashells or driftwood, at national parks and many state parks. The Endangered Species Act makes it illegal to own animal parts from endangered species. There are state, federal, and inter-national laws against collecting or transporting wildlife. Most people don't realize this, but except for a few special circumstances it's illegal to possess the feather of a wild bird. Ray has operated under Academy permits as a Field Associate since the 1960s. Before that, there were very few laws against collecting animals and animal parts. Ray's bones, even the ones he has at home, are legally part of the Academy's collection and all of them will eventually go to the Academy.

For thirty-two years Ray's day job was teaching biology, human anatomy, and physiology at Fremont High. Students from the 1960s and 1970s still keep in touch with him. Unsurprisingly, a number of them have become biologists. Ray's classroom was unusual for its time and would be even more unusual today. He shared his finds freely with his students, who must have thought he was pretty cool. Other students dissect frogs in school, but Ray's students dissected dolphins, pythons, monkeys, even a giraffe neck. I saw photographs of a class dissecting a male chimpanzee as large as a person. (Ray says only the 12th graders did the dissections themselves; the 10th graders watched as Ray did it and narrated.) The room was full of class pets and visiting animals, including bats and lots of reptiles. Bones were everywhere. Ray would show slide shows of his collecting trips. No wonder his students remember him.

Ray's motivation for collecting is mostly aesthetic. He thinks of bones as magnificent pieces of sculpture. His collections are also catalogs of skull diversity. You learn more about an animal from its skull than from any other body part. When you have so many versions of the same thing, in particular the 2,000 California sea lion skulls (the world's largest collec-tion), it becomes possible to compare their subtle differences. Charles Darwin's theory of evolution depends on two ideas: variation and natural selection. Everyone knows about the natural selection part ("survival of the fittest") but it's easy to forget that without random *variation* between indi-viduals in a species, natural selection would have nothing to work on. The sea lion skulls are a library of sea lion variation. They form a large enough data set for marine mammal experts to use to look for statistical patterns of trauma and disease. Scientists come to Ray to analyze these skulls. For instance, who knew that sea lions can suffer from temporo-mandibular joint disorder? Now we do.

Today Ray sets up temporary exhibits and workshops for teachers, donors, members, and special events at the Academy. There will be a permanent exhibit of his skulls on the main floor of the museum when the special exhibit is over. It's unlikely that any one person will ever again assemble a collection like this. I learned from meeting Ray that given enough time, effort, and resources, a personal hobby or obsession can grow into a marvelous project that is appreciated by others. Also, that Ray's affiliation with the Academy was critical to his success.

3

Apply for Things

"Opportunity is missed by most people because it is dressed in overalls and looks like work."
—attributed to Thomas Edison

A few years ago I was one of two dozen lucky teachers from across the United States to participate in a study tour of the Galapagos Islands through the Toyota International Teacher Program. We saw the famous wildlife that helped Charles Darwin form his ideas about evolution, visited local schools, and studied the archipelago's efforts to sustainably accommodate a growing population. The experience made me a better teacher of evolution and I had ideas while on the trip that are still paying dividends today. It was totally free. Toyota Motor Sales paid for everything, including our substitute teachers back home; they even gave us some spending money.

There are over three million school teachers in America. Most meet Toyota's eligibility requirements. The program was open to full-time teachers, public and private, in all subject areas and all grades. However, even though the program offered a free trip to the Galapagos and some high-quality professional development, only a few hundred teachers across the United States applied. That's about one one-hundredth of 1 percent of all eligible teachers.

Why so few? Most of those millions of teachers had never heard of the program. Some knew about it but weren't interested. Maybe some thought they couldn't leave their families for two weeks, or that their principals wouldn't support them, or that their students couldn't learn anything from a substitute teacher. Most of the rest thought, "That sounds great but writing essays and getting letters of recommendation is a lot of work and I don't have the time. Odds are I'll never get it; there must be thousands of people applying."

I had all those thoughts too, but something made me sit down and hammer out an application anyway. The Galapagos are an expensive place to travel to; I wasn't going to get there any other way. I had been teaching for eight years. I felt I had mostly mastered the job but was concerned about getting too static. My children were old enough to live without me for two weeks. Also, since I teach in a 9th and 10th grade blended academy at my school, I thought that our style of collaborative teaching and learning might get my application noticed a bit more than that of a typical teacher who works alone. I read the application forms carefully, and I tried to offer Toyota the outcomes it wanted. Anyway, the small risk I took (of wasted time and disappointment) paid off.

The two dozen teachers were all from different states. As we started to travel together around the islands, I noticed that some of them knew each other already. Each time I asked how this was, and I would get an answer like, "Oh, we were together two years ago in Korea." "We were in the same program three years ago in Saudi Arabia." I realized with a shock that there are other programs that send teachers on overseas trips for free, and that *the same few teachers apply to all of them.* I became one of those few.

The author at Darwin Station, Galapagos Islands. Photo by Michael Wing.

That was my big break. It was in the Galapagos that the idea came to me for our high altitude garden in the White Mountains, and I don't think I would have had it at home. The high altitude garden lead me to the bristlecone pines project and the artificial hypoliths project. Without the Galapagos experience, I wouldn't have heard of the National Science Foundation-sponsored PolarTREC program that sent me to Finland, and I probably wouldn't have been accepted by this program without the high altitude garden project to write about on my application. The Finland expedition, in turn, led to my work on the Point Reyes stone line.

Applying for grants, programs, and contests is like buying a lottery ticket, except with better odds. Millions of people in my state buy lottery tickets for which the odds of winning anything life-changing are virtually zero. Participation in these lotteries soars whenever the jackpot gets especially high. What people are really buying for their couple of bucks is the right to daydream. In the window of time between purchasing the ticket and finding out that you didn't win you can fantasize about what you would do with the money. But when you apply for programs and grants that you are eligible for, and that seem like a good fit with your interests and experience, the odds are not one in a million. I get between 25 percent and 50 percent of the things I apply for. It helps that I have a record of past achievements and that I teach in an academy, and that I know how to read the application materials and figure out what they want, and that my school administrators support me. But my best asset is the taste of success. Having scored big with the Toyota program, no other application form seems onerous to me. I know how to submit a successful application, and I know that applying for things pays off even though I strike out sometimes. While I wait for the decision, I get to daydream like any lottery ticket holder, except I know the odds are pretty good.

A few people apply for things all the time and you should too. Don't be put off if you don't get them at first. Keep trying. The first time you get that acceptance, it will change your whole outlook on risk and reward, I promise.

What grants and programs should you apply for, and how do you learn about them? This depends on geography and your personal circumstances. As a science teacher in California, I have participated in the Toyota International Teacher Program, the National Science Foundation's PolarTREC Program, NASA's Spaceward Bound Program, a National Geographic Society Waitt Grant, the Houghton Mars Project, The ING

Unsung Heroes Awards Program, The National Oceanic and Atmospheric Administration's Ocean Guardian School Program and Teacher at Sea Program, Earthwatch's Teach Earth Program, the California Fertilizer Foundation School Garden Grants Program, the Pacific Gas & Electric Company's Solar Schools Program, the Toshiba America Foundation's grants program, and others. If you are a historian in New York and not a teacher your list is going to look different. Ask around and do some research. Programs come and go, and details and websites change. The Toyota program that got me started down this road is no longer active, but discontinued programs have a way of being revived.

Once you gain experience, don't assume that you should only apply for programs tailor-made for people like you. The National Geographic Society Waitt grant that sent me to the Arctic was not intended for teachers at all, but for full-time researchers getting started in their careers, Ph.D. candidates, and post-doctoral fellows. I applied anyway (it was a long shot) but I'm glad I did.

What does a successful application look like? At the end of this book are the texts of some successful grant and program applications I have made. These offer an idea of what kinds of prompts and questions you will be asked and what sorts of answers are expected. One was to the National Science Foundation-funded PolarTREC Professional Development Program for Teachers, administered by the Arctic Research Consortium of the United States. This is the program that sent me to Alaska and Finland. A second is a research proposal I made for a National Geographic Society's Waitt Grant. I used the money to do fieldwork in the Arctic and Namibia. I have also included my school's application to the National Oceanic and Atmospheric Administration's Ocean Guardian School Program. We use this money to go on field trips to the Point Reyes National Seashore.

Most applications to organized programs, such as teacher travel programs, ask for similar things. First, they want contact information: your name, address, email, affiliation, and so on. They may ask for demographic information like your gender, race, and citizenship. There will be questions about your education, experience, and background. You will get a chance to list any certifications, licenses, registrations, publications, awards, and honors you may have. There will be a question about your motivation— why do you want to participate? "To get some free travel!" is never a good enough answer. It's better to demonstrate with specific evidence that you have a long-standing interest in the subject of the program, and a track record of building on experiences like this. You will probably be asked about what plans you have for sharing your experience with others. Since technology skills like blogging and using social media are a part of doing effective outreach, they will want to know that you have some of these skills. You will probably be asked about your health and physical condition, especially if outdoor activities are involved. Participation in most organized programs requires teamwork and being a good sport in a group situation. Be ready to provide specific examples of your teamwork skills. Be ready to provide the names and contact information of a few influential people you can use as references. You may have to ask them to write letters of recommendation. When I have to ask people for letters of recommendation, I sometimes offer to write the letter myself. That saves my recommender time and effort. He or she just has to sign it. Plus, I write good letters of recommendation.

The key to success with program and grant applications is to put yourself in the shoes of the organization giving out the goodies. Every organization has objectives and wants to obtain them efficiently and well. Your own interests and goals will not overlap 100 percent with theirs, but if you want your application to be successful you really do have to promise them everything they want. This may mean, for example, developing a much more detailed outreach plan than you initially felt like implementing or making lots of measurements on the effectiveness of the outreach you do. Administrators of grants and programs love reportable numbers.

For grant applications, some of the required information is similar to that for programs: your contact information, biographical information, and education. You are pitching an idea of your own and a request for a specific amount of money, not just your participation in an activity organized by others, so there are differences. You will be prompted for a project title and an abstract, which is a one-paragraph summary of the proposed project. It will need to have specific start- and end-dates, a specific amount of money requested, and maybe details on the geographic location in which it will be done. You may be asked about previous grants you have obtained, and about your plan for disseminating the results of your work.

Other people may be involved, either as participants in the project or as non-participating officers of the institution you are affiliated with: a university, school, arts organization, historical society, etc. Many grants are not really made to individuals, but to institutions. You may have to get your boss(es) to sign off on your grant proposal. If there are other participants in the project, you will probably be asked for their qualifications, educational backgrounds, and contact information as well.

The main body of your grant proposal will introduce and describe the project and its objectives and make a case that it is important. What is already known? What's already been done? What will you do? Why does it matter and to whom? You have to answer the question "so what?" with a powerful and compelling rationale. You should identify the specific audience or target population that will be affected. You also have to show with convincing self-promotion that you are the right person to do this work. It can help to recruit other experts to work with you or advise you.

The heart of any project is a timeline and a budget, and your granting agency will want details on both. Some project milestones are going to depend on others, so plan all that out: the meetings, division of labor, schedule, and due dates. You will probably have to make an itemized budget with things like equipment and supplies, transportation expenses, food and lodging, postage and other communication expenses, registration and permit fees, and maybe a stipend for yourself. Your time is worth something. You may be asked to itemize matching funds and in-kind donations from other sources. Don't panic if some of your plans, expenses, goals, and dates have to change while the project is underway. This is normal. Your granting agency won't be outraged as long as you give them something like what you promised.

If your project involves building an outdoor structure, studying wildlife or native plants, geological sampling, archaeology, human remains, or using human or animal test subjects, there will be special regulations you need to follow. You may have to get permits, follow protocols, and do specialized follow-up reporting. You granting agency will want to know that you are on top of that.

Don't be shocked by this, but successful applicants sometimes propose to do work that is already partly done, or even mostly done. Then they use the money to advance their *next* project to a stage where it is ready to attract funding. The granting agency gets what it was promised and the money is used for activities similar to the proposed ones, so it isn't considered fraudulent.

. . . .

Profile: Lindsay Knippenberg, polar traveler

Lindsay is another one of those three million school teachers in America. I met Lindsay when I was in Fairbanks, Alaska, being trained in field communications and polar studies with the PolarTREC program. I was headed for northern Finland, she for Antarctica. (I was a finalist for the Antarctic expedition she went on and had hoped for her spot, but that's water under the bridge.) PolarTREC was her first unusual professional development experience as a teacher, but she has done more in the years since, so I called her up to ask her about her adventures.

Lindsay attended Michigan State University and the University of Michigan and earned degrees in biology and environmental science. Her first job was teaching science at South Lake High School, near Detroit. She taught there for seven years. Lindsay is passionate about service learning and the environment, and she had her inner-city students do projects in their community. She organized beach cleanups on the shores of Lake St. Claire. She had her students label storm drains with the warning "No Dumping—Drains to Lake." Her students designed stickers that say "Lake Safe" and she got them manufactured. Her students visited local stores and arranged to put the "Lake Safe" stickers on products like fertilizers that are low in phosphorus or that release nitrogen slowly. Choosing these products reduces pollution in Lake St. Claire and Lake Erie.

Lindsay applied to several teacher programs early in her teaching career, including the National Oceanic and Atmospheric Administration (NOAA)'s Teacher at Sea program. She didn't get accepted. "I just didn't have the experience yet," she says. She kept trying and succeeded with PolarTREC.

She joined an expedition lead by scientists from Montana State University studying microorganisms in Antarctic glacier ice. She visited their lab in Montana before her trip to Antarctica. The expedition itself took two months! The National Science Foundation paid for her substitute teacher and all her expenses. First they flew to New Zealand, and from there they took a C-17 military cargo plane to the U. S. Antarctic Program's McMurdo Station on Ross Island. At McMurdo there was lots of training: how to drive light vehicles on the ice and the famous "Happy Camper" emergency survival school where she got to dig a snow cave outside and sleep in it overnight. There was also lots of packing and planning and waiting for good flying weather. When the good weather arrived, she and her team were airlifted by helicopter to one of the McMurdo dry valleys.

Most people believe that Antarctica is completely covered by ice. Actually, there are ice-free areas on the Antarctic mainland and Lindsay's valley is one of them. It is a stark desert landscape, with no visible sign of life. They camped for almost a month in small tents on the shore of Lake Bonney, which is permanently frozen and salty. The sun was always up. Temperatures, with wind chill, got as low as -40 degrees Fahrenheit. Nearby, the Taylor Glacier ends in a vertical wall of ice. Lindsay and her team cut a tunnel into the wall of ice using chain saws. They were after samples of bacteria that live in the ice.

It might come as a surprise that there are bacteria under the ice in Antarctica, but to date every environment on earth that is capable of supporting life has been found to actually support life, no matter how extreme the conditions. Water freezes at 32 degrees Fahrenheit, but the freezing point is lowered quite a bit if salts are present, and when fresh water freezes, the salts tend to end up in little pockets of very briny water. So even though it's very cold inside the glacier there is liquid water present in places, and there are also layers of sediments frozen into it that provide sources of organic carbon, sulfur compounds, and other energy sources. Nobody doubted that bacteria would be found there. The question was, are they actually active? Are they eating, growing, and reproducing in the ice, or are they just waiting for better days? It turns out that bacteria are indeed living out their complete life cycles there, just very slowly.

Lindsay's jobs at camp included operating the chain saw, carrying blocks of ice out of the tunnel, packing and unpacking, collecting scientific samples, and posting journal entries and photos from the field to her PolarTREC blog where it was read by classrooms all over the United States. She used a satellite phone with a solar charger. The team recovered temperature data loggers they had left in the ice two years earlier. They collected samples of ice, mud, bacteria, and gases from the glacier to analyze back in the lab in Montana. She also performed a number of simple experiments online for her students at home, who analyzed the data in their classrooms. For example, she did a bacterial growth experiment and experiments on the melting rates of different ice samples, and she measured the conductivity of the melted ice samples.

While she was still in Antarctica, Lindsay applied for an Albert Einstein Distinguished Educator Fellowship. This program brings about thirty teachers annually from all over the United States to Washington, D.C., and places them in federal offices to do policy and public outreach work for a year. A stipend and living expenses are provided. Lindsay explains that the Einstein Fellow acts as a "voice of reason" and reality-check in his or her office, which usually has no other teachers, although it does things that affect education. Because of her interest in aquatic ecosystems, Lindsay got to work for NOAA. She moved to Washington and worked on the intersection of public education with NOAA's oceanographic missions. These included making presentations about NOAA resources, lesson plans, and professional development opportunities at conferences like the National Science Teachers Association meetings, American Geophysical Union meetings, and local Washington D.C. area schools. The American Geophysical Union meetings allowed her to reconnect with her Montana State University teammates several times. She also developed education content for NOAA's website and reviewed applications for grants and programs including, ironically, the Teacher at Sea program that had once turned her down.

One of the perks of the Einstein Fellowship was that she got to be a Teacher at Sea after all. She joined the NOAA research ship *Oscar Dyson* in Unalaska, in the Aleutian Islands, for a two-week cruise to the Bering Sea. The purpose of the trip was to conduct a salmon survey in international waters. Lindsay and the ship's staff netted salmon and made measurements on their sizes, genetics, condition, maturity, gender ratios, stomach contents, etc. As in Antarctica, she posted journal entries and photographs of what they were doing to NOAA's website, where it was followed by classrooms around the country.

The Einstein Fellowship is meant to last one year, but South Lake High School was cutting staff and Lindsay lacked seniority. NOAA asked her to stay on for a second year, so she did. She has since returned to full-time classroom teaching, but still works for NOAA as a contractor, through Tech Global, Inc., developing content for NOAA's website.

Lindsay is developing water quality projects at her new school and is continuing to explore oceanography. She recently participated in the Monterey Bay Aquarium and Research Institute's EARTH Program, which was held in Hawaii. This is an all-expenses-paid workshop for ten teachers from around the United States and ten from the local venue (Hawaii, in this case) who work together for two weeks to develop oceanography curricula and learn about the marine environment. They are paid a stipend.

Since she has such success in applying for programs, and has also reviewed other people's applications, I asked Lindsay for some pointers. She laughed and said, "Answer the questions! We're using a rubric." This may seem obvious, but questions on application packets frequently contain several parts and when you sit down to answer them you should put yourself in the position of a reviewer with a checklist. Did you thoroughly answer all the parts of each question? She also remarked that programs like Teacher at Sea or PolarTREC typically get at least ten times as many applicants as there are spaces in it. To boost your odds above 10 percent, you have to stand out. She said to think about what makes you unique, and say that. Your genuine enthusiasm has to come through; it won't work to fake it with boilerplate prose. One thing that will make you look unique and stand out is to have a cool, ongoing project. When Lindsay started teaching she had no particular advantage over the three million teachers who didn't get to go to Antarctica. Her persistence paid off, and the service learning projects she did with her South Lake High School students helped her get noticed.

4

Travel with Purpose

"It is not worth the while to go round the world to count the cats in Zanzibar."
—Henry David Thoreau, *Walden*

Counting the cats in Zanzibar is exactly what Hackademics[1] do. It can be worthwhile. Most travel literature is about hotels, restaurants, and seeing the tourist sites. There's more to travel than that. Travel with a sense of mission is more satisfying and more transformative than travel without one, and you still get to experience the hotels, restaurants, and tourist sites. The mission might be to attend a conference or to do location-specific research, whether it is scientific fieldwork, archaeology, examining museum collections, or reading texts in library archives.

On my first morning in Namibia, I was wide awake at 4 AM (jet lag) so I went out for a walk. Outside the bunkhouse of the Gobabeb Research & Training Centre the fog from the Atlantic Ocean was thick, chilly, and damp and it smelled like seaweed, although we were fifty miles from the coast. I picked my way across the yard and crossed a wire fence. Ahead of me in the dark were the trees lining the dry bed of the Kuiseb river. As my eyes adjusted, I could make out many kinds of animal tracks in the sand and big curly seed pods from the trees lying on the ground. I went a mile or two up the river, crossed the river bed, and started to climb the first sand dune. It had ripple marks from the wind, and it too was covered with trackways of all sizes, from beetles and rodents to fox-sized animals to big herbivores. I was joined by a South African journalist, a member of our party, who got up to see the sunrise. We heard a horrible loud noise suddenly nearby in the fog, and we jumped. My mind raced as I reassured myself that this area has no large carnivores—no lions, no hyenas. It turned out to be a donkey.

---

1 A neologism I use for people who have creative academic projects like those a professor might undertake, but who don't have the resources or status of a professor.

We climbed to the top of the first large dune and sat to watch the sun rise over Africa. The fog was gone. The dunes were an impossibly golden-orange color and the low-light angle cast crazy shadows. From hundreds of feet up, we looked north across the gravely plain of the Namib–Naukluft National Park, and south across a sea of dunes. I took some pictures.

On the way back across the river, colorful African songbirds were twittering and flitting back and forth in the sun. Weaverbirds were clinging to the outsides of their nests, which look like burlap sacks hanging from the branches. A delicious and hearty breakfast was waiting for us at the dining hall: Middle-class Namibians eat like Germans used to. I was deliriously happy, and the real business of my day hadn't even started yet. I was there to deploy my hypolith project, and I had looked forward to this for a long time. I was there with a team of NASA scientists.

I have other great memories, from the Galapagos, Finland, Alaska, the Arctic, and the Emirates, like the time a stranger in Madinat Zayed invited a few of us scientists to visit his camel stables. I was expecting some place dusty and smelling like animals, but instead we sat on rugs and cushions outside under the stars, with a big wood fire and a wide-screen TV. Servants brought us dates and coffee, hot milk with ginger, and water pipes, while we talked about world affairs for hours and ate a delicious dinner of chicken biryani with our fingers. Or my day off in the Galapagos when a teacher from Arizona and I bicycled across the island in the fog and went swimming with sea turtles on a deserted beach. There were the days I dressed up in fox skins like a Neolithic hunter-gatherer at the Kierikki Stone Age Centre in northern Finland and taught classes of visiting 5th graders how to make slate beads. There was the time I hopped from airport to airport in the Canadian Arctic, headed for Devon Island. Ticket fares and weather delays made it sensible to crisscross the continent and sleep in places like Yellowknife, Iqaluit, Arctic Bay, and Resolute on the way. These experiences were all the more special because in each of these places I had some work to do relating to research or education. For me, there's something deflating about simply being a tourist. Local people treat you better, too, if they know you're there for a specific reason, and you get to see places that tourists don't get to see. Having a project makes for a much more authentic travel experience.

If you're a teacher, there are programs that will send you somewhere interesting for free professional development, including the PolarTREC program mentioned earlier. The U. S. State Department offers some, and

The author in Namibia. Photo by Michael Wing.

there are several different programs with the word "Fulbright" in the title. There's a nonprofit organization called the Institute of International Education that administers some of these programs, even where another agency is paying for them. In all, I've identified over two dozen outfits that send teachers overseas (or out to sea) for free. Program details change, and websites come and go, so the best thing is just to search online, but there is also a list included at the end of this book.

When I travel like this I always keep a daily journal, and usually a blog. So many new experiences are happening to me so quickly that if I don't write things down several times a day I will lose some of it. I like to carry a little spiral-bound, waterproof notebook and a pencil with me wherever I go to write down places, names, data, experiences, and ideas as they come to me in the course of the day. Then in the evening, if I have internet access, I use my notes to write a daily blog on some specific topic. The first time I did this I blogged on PolarTREC's website; then I used Blogspot. Now I have my own site.

It's always a good idea to read some of the literature of the place you are visiting before and during your trip. To prepare for Namibia, I read *The Sheltering Desert* by Henno Martin and *The Namib: Natural History of an Ancient Desert* by Mary Seely. While I read the latter book, I had no idea that I would eventually meet the writer and co-author a scientific paper with her. From both books I gained an appreciation for how patchy the rain there is, and how much depends on it. Everyone knows that deserts are dry, but few people realize how variable they are in time and space. When I went to the United Arab Emirates, I read Wilfred Thesiger's *Arabian Sands*. Thesiger traveled the Empty Quarter in the 1940s, visiting many of the same places I did. It is staggering to see how much has changed in one lifetime. People whose grandparents lived in homemade tents drive sports utility vehicles down new highways, own apartments in glamorous high-rise buildings, and vacation in London and Paris.

When I went to Finland, I read the *Kalevala*, Finland's national epic. I absolutely loved it. You learn something about a country's character from reading its most important book. The *Kalevala* is not like the *Odyssey* or *Beowulf*. Its characters are local heroes, not acting on a national or international scene. All the action takes place in the "Kaleva district," a mythical place you won't find on the map, and in "Northland," which is a few days travel from the Kaleva district (although some people believe that these two places stand for Finland and Lapland). There is very little fighting. More than once when a fight is imminent somebody opts for negotiation or magic instead. What fighting there is, is personal. It's usually not organized enough or premeditated enough to be war. Instead, large sections of the book consist of really detailed descriptions of housework: how to bake bread, brew beer, forge iron, carve skis, clean the house, prepare the sauna, etc. There's advice about how to get along with the in-laws. There are also spells and incantations against illness, wounds, and bears. In the *Kalevala*, every second verse repeats the verse before it. That is because they come from an ancient oral tradition and were meant to be sung out loud by two singers working together. The lead singer recites a few words, and his assistant immediately adds a few more which repeat and affirm what the lead singer has just said. I digress, but the point is that I never would have read this book or come to love it if I hadn't gone to Finland for a reason that had nothing to do with literature. So, read the great books of the places you visit.

Don't neglect to invite yourself to a local school, if you travel when school is in session. Usually, all you have to do is contact the principal or headmaster, explain who you are, and request a visit. Somebody will show you around. You may get put in front of a classroom full of students for an impromptu talk about life at home, or about the project that brings you there. Meeting students and teachers from other places is always rewarding. I've been to schools in South America, India, Africa, and Europe. You should do this even if you're not a teacher, if you're in a rural or under-served area that doesn't get many visitors.

Besides free programs for teachers, there is another universe of more commercial travel programs where you get to bring some of your students with you. These programs are not free, at least not for the students. Usually, if a teacher rounds up a certain number of students paying full fare, the teacher himself or herself goes for free. EF Educational Tours is an example; ACIS is another.

. . . .

Profile: Kevin Witte, geographer

Earth scientists tell each other "the best geologist is the one who has seen the most rocks." Is the best geographer the one who has seen the most places? What about geography teachers? Kevin Witte teaches high school geography and world history in the town where he grew up: Kearney, Nebraska, a city of about 30,000 on the Platte River and Interstate 80. It is several hours drive from larger places like Omaha and Lincoln. I first met Kevin in the Galapagos where he and I were on a study tour hosted by the Toyota International Teacher Program. It was my first experience like that. Kevin had already been to Italy, Japan, Greece, Egypt, Saudi Arabia, and South Africa on similar programs. A few of the other teachers on the Galapagos trip were also veterans of these programs; Kevin already knew one or two of them, even though we were all from different states. Since then he has done more programs like these.

What programs? There is a list at the end of this book and Kevin has participated in many of them. They have names like the Fulbright Memorial Fund to Japan, Aramco's Educators to Saudi Arabia Program, the Fulbright-Hayes Summer Seminars Abroad, the Korea Society's Summer Fellowship in Korean Studies for American Educators, and the Goethe Institute's Transatlantic Outreach Program. Some of these are no longer in opera-

Nebraska teacher Kevin Witte in Svalbard. Photo by Kevin Witte.

tion, but new ones are getting created at the same rate that old ones get discontinued. At any given time there are about two dozen such programs. Most of these pay all of the teacher's expenses.

For Kevin, it started in his second year of teaching when he applied to go to Italy through the Fulbright Classics Summer Seminars program sponsored by the U.S. State Department. "My principal handed me an ad from a magazine that he had read. I didn't really know how much of a chance I had," Kevin recalled. He applied, and was selected as an alternate, in case somebody else cancelled. A few weeks before this two-month program began, somebody cancelled. Suddenly, Kevin's summer was fully booked. It changed his life, because Kevin had been thinking about leaving high school teaching to enter a full-time Ph.D. program in history. Half of his fellow participants in Italy were teachers like himself, and half were graduate students. Spending the summer with them, seeing the ancient sites and getting his fill of the classics and the academic life, Kevin realized that he didn't have to stop teaching to do what he wanted. He realized high school was the perfect setting for him. He did go on to earn a M.A. in history from the University of Nebraska at Kearney, but he did it part time and still teaches at Kearney High.

Different trips had different highlights. Kevin on Japan: "There were over 200 teachers in the program, and they took us in small groups to different parts of the country, so it was kind of neat to share our different experiences. Also, I had a home stay—with not much English—it was definitely out of my comfort zone." He took some students from Kearney High School to Greece through ACIS: "Some of the kids earned the money to pay their entire way themselves. That was kind of neat. Also, we took the overnight ferry from Greece to Italy. That's a big deal for Nebraskans." On Egypt: "We had great connections with the Egyptian Fulbright Scholars. One morning we met with someone from the Arab League about Israel/Palestine issues and then that evening we talked with Israel's ambassador to Egypt for the other perspective. We got to talk with real diplomats." Saudi Arabia: "It was a pretty fascinating place to visit. It's very hard to go there by yourself. We were completely supervised the whole time. The hotels and meals were first class; we were pampered. There was a real effort to dispel misconceptions and cultural misunderstandings. The Saudis want to be understood."

Kevin didn't have to tell me about the Galapagos trip, because I did it with him. We saw lots of tame wildlife, and we visited schools. The focus of the trip was on sustainability. Modern tourism has brought a population explosion to these islands. The number of residents has risen from about 300 to well over 30,000 in just a few decades, because of the jobs provided by tourism and nonprofit conservation and scientific organizations. A worker in the Galapagos can earn several times what he or she can in mainland Ecuador. This results in invasive species, a construction boom, illegal immigration, waste management challenges, water shortages, and social friction. So the Galapagos are a microcosm of the rest of the world. Like me, Kevin left the islands more interested in sustainability than before. Some of the things he does in his classes have taken on an environmental focus as a result of that trip.

After we parted ways, Kevin continued taking study tours for teachers. On Korea: "We went to a Hyundai shipyard on the coast, and to Seoul. It was not part of the program to go to the demilitarized zone, but I went a couple of times on free days. I was taken on a tour of the border zone by an American soldier." China: "There was some political trouble and the government was blocking Twitter. Some of the concrete pavement from the Beijing Olympics was already breaking." Germany: "We went to Germany while the World Cup was being held in South Africa. Germans are not very nationalistic, except during the World Cup. Then there are flags everywhere." On Svalbard, in Norway's Arctic: "There were only six teachers in the program that year. A lot of what I do is history, but I fell in love with the Arctic! I was blown away. I want to go back. They put us in staff cabins on the ship. Any time we could help out, we jumped in." Istanbul: "We studied Istanbul's origin from ancient Greek times, to Rome, to Byzantium, to the Ottomans, to modern Turkey. Leading classical, Byzantine, and Ottoman historians traveled with us—experts. We were there during the Gezi Park protests." When I spoke with Kevin recently, he was preparing for a trip, with high school students, to Malaysia and Singapore with the American Youth Leadership Program.

Organizations like these wouldn't keep sending Kevin abroad unless it benefited his students. He says, "There's always a way for me to weave it—anywhere I go—into the classroom. Travel allows me to build a lot of depth, a lot of personal experiences, into AP world history and geography." Besides these classes, Kevin has designed and taught an elective class called "International Wealth and Poverty." Kearney is mostly middle class, but Kevin has seen both extremes. One of the poorest places Kevin has been to is right in the same time zone with Kearney: the Pine Ridge Indian Reservation in South Dakota.

Recently the Milken Family Foundation awarded Kevin an unexpected prize of $25,000. The program is called the Milken Educator Award, and, like the Nobel Prize, you can't apply for it or nominate anyone. They come looking for you. The award sometimes gets called the "Oscars of Teaching." It is for early and mid-career teachers. There were 33 awards given that year nationwide. Kevin was the only one from Nebraska. The award ceremony was held in the gym in front of the whole school. The Governor of Nebraska was there. The Foundation cited Kevin's "contagious curiosity," his students' high AP test scores, the Wealth & Poverty class, student-lead discussions, and his students' accomplishments at the University of Nebraska History Day competition.

Kevin says, "I teach high school students, but I do see myself as an academic. I like to pursue my own understanding of the world I live in. I love that I have a job and a supportive family that allows for that." Kevin has consulted for the Nebraska Social Studies Standards Revision Working Group and continues to work on global education projects across the state with a group called the Malaika Foundation, so his trips influence (in a small way) what all Nebraskans learn. It is typical of Kevin and his Midwestern milieu that he doesn't advertise this fact or any of his accomplishments or awards. His school website lists the courses he teaches and says that he is the head coach of the ninth grade boys basketball team.

• •

A home in Somerset, England, obtained through the Homelink International home exchange organization. Photo by Michael Wing.

Home exchanges

One way to live cheaply and authentically in a foreign country is to do a home exchange. My family and I have done it twice, once to Norway and once to England. Although the home exchange concept was invented for teachers and their families traveling during the summer, anyone can do it at any time of the year. We used a service called Homelink International. To join Homelink, you pay an annual fee that gives you access to a database of thousands of households around the world. You post a listing of your own home with a few photos and you indicate where you want to go and when. You look at the listings in the country you want to visit for a good match. If you find one, you contact that person or family through the organization. The most common deal is a straight swap, done simultaneously: my house and car for your house and car for several weeks. No money changes hands. It's likely you'll never meet the other party face-to-face, although your neighbors will.

Lending your house and car to strangers while you're out of town might seem risky, and some people can't bear the thought of it. In reality, though, almost everybody who joins home exchange organizations is decent and responsible. Negative experiences in which someone's house or belongings are seriously damaged or stolen are quite rare. The kind of people who offer their homes to others are optimistic and trusting, and people who are like that tend not to abuse the trust of others.

A home exchange is especially convenient when both parties are families with children. You show up at your home away from home, and the beds are the right size. There are toys and children's books. The books may be in another language, but that's educational. Neighbors bring their children over to check you out, and they invite you to do things. Our house in Norway came with some pet rabbits that we fed while the other family was in America. My son came to love feeding "his" rabbits at the end of each day.

Home exchanges also save you a lot of money over commercial travel arrangements. Not only is your lodging free, and maybe the use of a car, but since you have access to a full kitchen you spend less money at restaurants. Norway is an expensive country, and we couldn't have stayed there for almost a month if we were paying for a hotel every night.

Having a home base in another country changes the way you travel, too. You spend more time exploring the area where you live and less time in transit. Norway is big. There are large parts of it we never saw, but we came to know the beautiful Gudbrandsdalen, the historic valley which includes Lillehammer, intimately. Similarly, when we lived in England, we spent nearly all of our time in Somerset, Wiltshire, Avon, and Devon. This area richly rewards a close look.

· ·

Profile: William Schmoker, birder

Bill Schmoker has a master's degree from the University of Colorado and has taught earth science for over twenty years at Centennial Middle School in Boulder, Colorado. A few years ago he applied to the PolarTREC Program because, living inland, he thought some oceanography experience would help with his teaching. The first time he didn't get in; he was successful on his second try. Bill is an active birder and photographer, so his experience with photojournalism and blogging probably helped him get accepted. Some PolarTREC expeditions are on oceanographic ships, and he landed a spot on one of them. "I had never slept on a ship before that," he says. "I was out at sea for five weeks. It rounded me out."

His expedition on the United States Coast Guard icebreaker *Healy* was intended to identify the edge of the continental shelf in the Arctic Ocean. This area is rich in natural resources including oil, natural gas, and fish. It was a joint project with Canada, cruising along the border between American and Canadian waters in the Beaufort Sea. The *Healy* was accompanied by a Canadian ship, the *Louis S. St-Lawrence*. They left Dutch Harbor, Alaska, with a crew of scientists from the United States Geological Survey. Another teacher, a participant in the NOAA Teacher at Sea program, was also on board. Heading north, they crossed the Arctic Circle and entered sea ice.

Besides posting daily blogs to the PolarTREC website, Bill participated fully in the scientific work on board. He stood geophysical watches, which means staying up all night monitoring the sonar systems to make sure they are working properly. The scientific party also collected seawater samples for an ocean acidification study, measured the salinity and temperature of the water from the surface to the sea floor, deployed meteorological drift buoys, and collected lots of sediment samples from the sea floor. They made really detailed maps of the sea floor, and of the layers of mud and rock beneath it.

One of the interesting things Bill saw on board the *Healy* was methane hydrates. Under pressure, natural gas and water can combine to form a solid compound that looks like ice but fizzes and bubbles when you bring it up to the surface of the sea. Methane hydrates matter for two reasons. They are potentially valuable as fossil fuels. But, as unstable solids that release methane gas, they contribute to global warming. Global warming, in turn, can release more methane hydrates since even a very slight rise in seawater temperatures can make them de-gas. Since they can only exist under pressure, few people besides scientists and petroleum engineers have ever seen them.

The expedition was about sea floor geology, not wildlife, but a birder like Bill wasn't going to miss an opportunity to see some wildlife, photograph it, and write about it. He left his big camera rig at home, but he was still very well equipped by most people's standards. On shore in Dutch Harbor, he watched ptarmigans, puffins, and bald eagles. At sea he saw shearwaters, gulls, petrels, and murres, as wells as polar bears, ringed seals, and minke whales. "Whether you're on a birding trip or not, there's birds around," he says. (Bill's Colorado license plate says "BRDPICS.")

Since the expedition went into late August, Bill had to miss the first three weeks of class! You can bet he was up late at nights working to introduce himself remotely to his new crop of middle schoolers and coordinating with his substitute teacher to ensure a good start to the year. It must have felt odd at first to the students to have a teacher who was somewhere else, but it also gave Bill a lot of credibility with them. Students like to know that their teacher is an expert.

After the trip, his U. S. Geological Survey colleagues invited Bill to their lab in California to help analyze some of the sediment cores they had collected. Buried in the mud, they found cold seep clams—part of a dark ecosystem that depends on the chemical energy of hydrocarbons, oxygen, and hydrogen sulfide under the ocean floor. They also found pebbles from far away, presumably transported and dropped by floating ice. The next year PolarTREC invited him back to Fairbanks, Alaska, to help train the new cohort of teachers heading out to the Arctic and Antarctic.

Bill's Arctic travels weren't over, because then he applied to become a National Geographic Society Grosvenor Teacher Fellow. The National Geographic Society partners with Lindblad Expeditions to place teachers on some of their seagoing expeditions to the Arctic, all expenses paid. The goal of this professional development program is to promote geographical literacy and climate change awareness. There's no doubt that Bill's PolarTREC experience helped him get the fellowship. "Once you have done one or two of these applications, they get easier," he says. Before the expedition, the national Geographic Society flew Bill to Washington, D.C., for a few days for some pre-trip training. He met Gilbert Grosvenor, the Chairman Emeritus of the National Geographic Society after whom the program is named.

His ship this time was the *National Geographic Explorer.* He flew to Reykjavik, Iceland, to meet it and cruised up Iceland's scenic west coast, with its thousand years of Nordic history. Then they crossed the Denmark Strait, rounded Greenland's southern tip and made their way up the fjord-indented west coast of Greenland. Bill was technically "staff" on the ship but not formally a guide, naturalist, or photographer. He mingled with the passengers and engaged with them about the history and natural history of the places they visited. A few children were among the passengers (*National Geographic* calls them "young explorers") and Bill and a second

Grosvenor Fellow improvised some special projects for them, like making a depth profile of the temperature and salinity of the seawater in a fjord. A message in a bottle was found, written in Icelandic, and Bill helped the kids document it, answer it, and throw it back into the sea.

Bill is considering making a bid for the NOAA Teacher at Sea program in a year or two, but meanwhile he travels a lot on land as a birder. Bill is a member of the American Birding Association (ABA) and the Colorado Field Ornithologists and he teaches workshops, classes, and summer camps with both organizations on birding, photography, and ornithology. These include the ABA's Institute for Field Ornithology and Young Birder programs. He has also taught for the Nature Conservancy (about sand-hill cranes), the Boulder County Nature Association, and in the Audubon Society of Greater Denver's Master Birder Program. He helps train the Master Birders. This takes him all over the lower 48 states; for example, he has taught at Camp Avocet in Delaware. Sometimes the ABA pays for his travel. As an optics representative for Nikon (a "Nikon Birding ProStaff"), he speaks ten or twelve times per year at birding clubs or festivals. Nikon gives him gear and pays his expenses. He serves on the state records committee, keeping Colorado's bird list accurate. He is a judge for the ABA Young Birder of the Year award.

Bill used to write a column for the ABA newsletter called "Geared for Birding" and he still blogs for the ABA. He has written articles for *Colorado Birds*, the Colorado Field Ornithologists' quarterly journal. He wrote a chapter in a book titled "Good Birders Don't Wear White: 50 Tips from North America's Top Birders." But mostly he publishes photographs of birds. These appear in the ABA's *Birding Magazine*, *BirdWatching Magazine*, several British magazines, photographic field guides such as the *Smithsonian Field Guide to the Birds of North America*, and websites. He has photographed over 600 species.

Bill is also involved in the Cornell Lab of Ornithology's citizen science eBird project. eBird is an online tool for people to contribute their bird sightings to a database that is globally accessible. The project includes some vetting of questionable or unlikely reports. For example, if somebody reports seeing twenty pink flamingos in Colorado in January, Bill gets to review the report, maybe investigate it, and decide whether or not to include it.

Bill's university degrees are in geology and education, not biology. He is mostly self-taught in field ornithology. He sees middle-school teaching as his real job, and birding as a self-funding hobby. I asked him for advice. He says, "If you've got the adventure bug, you can combine it with teaching—and it will help you in your teaching."

5

Teach and Mentor

"They give the pupils something to do, not something to learn; and the doing is of such a nature as to demand thinking, or the intentional noting of connections; learning naturally results."
—John Dewey, *Democracy and Education*

If you have expertise to offer and you aren't already a teacher, you should find a way to pass along your skills and knowledge. That isn't hard to arrange. Every urban community has university extension courses, adult education classes, community colleges, and arts organizations. Many nonprofit organizations offer ways to teach classes and field institutes. If you're an artist, you may take on an apprentice, or if you're a scientist or a historian, you may get an intern. If your apprentice or intern is a college student, he or she should be able to get college credit for working with you.

The Point Reyes National Seashore Association, to go back to my local example, offers classes taught by dozens of instructors with very impressive biographies. Their spring/summer field institute catalog lists classes on drawing, painting, watercolor, writing, photography, basketry, tide pools, birds, butterflies, spiders, dragonflies, elk, wildflowers, nocturnal wildlife, edible plants, gardening, kayaking, hiking, maps, and history. The instructors get paid for teaching these classes, but it's not full-time work. They do it for love.

Not everyone who teaches enjoys it or does it well. Elementary and secondary school teachers at public schools at least have some training on how to do it; most other people don't. However, if you love your field, that enthusiasm frequently rubs off on students. It's a rare instructor who hasn't had a big impact on at least a few people.

Best teaching practices

The first class I ever taught on my own was an evening section of "Introduction to Oceanography" for San Diego City College. It was at a U.S. Navy training center. I was a twenty-five-year-old graduate student; the average age of my students was probably also twenty-five. They were enlisted men and women in the navy. Most of them had been to sea more than I had, but they didn't have the theoretical understanding of how the sea works that I did. Except for a field trip to some tide pools (the highlight of the class), I instinctively did what I had seen my own professors do: I lectured. I put a lot of time and care into crafting my lectures, and I was pretty proud of them. The students tolerated them politely. They were in the navy, after all. Some earned A's, some B's, some C's on the tests and assignments. Nobody failed. We went our separate ways afterwards.

If you're an experienced teacher, you can skip what follows. But if you're like I was then, your first class can be a more powerful teaching and learning experience for everyone than mine was. Lecturing, also known as "direct instruction," works fairly well for certain types of students, like me. It's not very effective for most. In the years since, I have taught every age group from ninth graders to graduate students and I am learning to do it better. There are lots of books and studies on what makes good teaching. Everyone has their list; here's mine.

First, you need to care about the subject. Your passion for it has to show. If you don't think it is really fascinating and super-important, leave the teaching of it to others. I once met a teacher at another school who taught world history to tenth graders. He told me he had trouble motivating them. "What can you expect?" he shrugged. "It's history." I seethed as I thought of my colleague Paul Grifo, who is the most charismatic, popular, and effective teacher I have ever seen. He has many tricks up his sleeve to get students to love history. He is theatrical, passionate, and never loses sight of his thesis that history is YOUR story—and it's how the world got into its present messy state of affairs! It's about power, morality, greed. He seems to take an article of faith from William Faulkner that the past is alive and not even past. That other guy just shouldn't have been teaching.

Like Paul Grifo, you need to sell your students on the relevance of what you have to teach them. In education, there is a common idea that the weaker and less motivated students need instruction that's dressed up to look "relevant," but that star students will be happy to study whether things appear relevant or not. This is not true. Star students appreciate being shown the relevance too, as long as it's genuine. Relevance can be practical ("This will get you a job"), but it can also be philosophical, as in "This helps explain your place in the cosmos." Spell out in detail how the subject matter is relevant to their lives. Don't assume they already can see this.

Most importantly, you should promote active and interactive learning. "Active" means stop talking already and get them doing things. Have them do projects, write stories and letters, measure things, do labs, graph data, make maps and models, enter contests, make videos, sing songs, and perform skits. "Interactive" means that to get these things done they need to work with each other and with the instructor. Offer them choices and offer them options to exercise their creativity.

You do owe it to your students to be entertaining. Nobody likes to be taught by a robot. Use humor (bad humor works fine), and let some of your personality and life experiences show through. Acting is a big part of teaching.

Some students are capable and some are incompetent. Some are nice and some are excessively needy. Some you like right away and some you have a hard time tolerating. Don't confuse academic ability with character or character with human dignity. Your students have intrinsic moral worth as humans, regardless of whether they make your life easier or harder. The hard-to-take ones don't really want to be like that; they just don't know any other way to be. They have less free will than you think. You need to find a way to respect everybody; all of your students will sense it if you don't.

Plan backwards: Decide first of all what it is you want them to be able to do. Then, design a few simple tests and assignments ("formative assessments") that you can give them along the way to see if they get it before it's too late. Based on the feedback you get from these, re-teach. The final exam (or "summative assessment") is no place for you to find out for the first time that they haven't acquired the skills you wanted them to acquire.

Plan each class period so as not to waste any of their time. Get into the habit of doing a two-minute review at the end of the period and/or at the start of the next period. Show your students examples of "A" work and also have them grade each other's work according to a specific rubric. Go into the classrooms of experienced, respected teachers and watch how they do things. You will pick up a few good tricks, but you will also realize just how slowly time crawls while you're being lectured at.

Take care of yourself! This means don't be a martyr. Our popular culture, especially television and Hollywood, loves the trope of the self-sacrificing teacher who works insanely hard for others who may not even appreciate it, and the teacher who puts his or her own legitimate needs on the back burner indefinitely. This is not sustainable. Set some limits, and also be sure to avail yourself of the perks you are entitled to that come with the job, like the opportunity to do some free travel.

Except for that field trip to the tide pools, I did none of these things the first time I taught. I just didn't know any better.

Adjunct teaching at universities

An adjunct professor teaches at a college or university, but the job has been defined by the institution as temporary and part-time. The word "adjunct" implies "supplemental," "auxiliary," and "not essential." In contrast to tenure-track jobs, adjunct teaching appointments at universities are not too hard to get if you have basic qualifications to teach the course. Some are never advertised, so ask around. Colleges and universities are using adjunct professors more and more often. Three-quarters of American college and university professors now have "adjunct" or otherwise non-tenure-track status. That doesn't mean that three-quarters of all classes are taught by them, because most adjuncts only teach a little, but it's a large proportion.

The good part about teaching as an adjunct is that inside the classroom it is the same experience as it is for a tenured or tenure-track professor. Your students will rarely know or care about the details of your employment contract with the university. They will judge you on the classroom experience, your personality, your expertise, and on the content of the class. A recent study at Northwestern University showed that students there actually learned more from adjunct professors than they did from tenured and tenure-track ones.

Outside the classroom it is different. Typically, you only get paid a few thousand dollars for teaching a course, so you would have to teach as much as three, four, five, or even more than five tenured professors to earn as much money as one of them. You can't do that anyway, because the institution won't allow it. There are no health benefits or retirement benefits, which is why the university doesn't want you to teach full-time. If you did, you would be eligible for benefits. You aren't given any of the resources for doing research or scholarship that real professors get, like laboratory space, start-up funds, or sabbaticals, and no research or scholarship is expected of you. You will have to pay for your own parking pass. Sometimes you don't even get a desk or a computer. Nobody will expect you to serve on committees, because you really don't belong to the institution. Your contract is short-term and comes up for renewal frequently. Your opportunities to mentor students outside of the classroom will be limited (because you aren't there that much) and you generally can't use your position to apply for grants and programs.

Don't imagine that teaching as an adjunct is a way to get your foot in the door with an academic department. When a full-time tenure-track position opens, it will be advertised nationally. Hundreds of highly qualified outsiders will apply for it, and you will not look that good compared to them.

Does that mean there is no appropriate role for adjunct teaching at universities? I think there is. For the university, the best use of adjunct professors is when there is a need to bring in the special expertise of a working professional in a situation where no tenure-track faculty member in the department is qualified to teach the class. In this model, the adjunct professors would be teaching the most advanced and specialized classes, like the time I taught a class on the geology and geochemistry of hazardous waste for the University of California at Berkeley. In practice, adjuncts do a lot of the introductory teaching because they're less expensive to the university and because the regular faculty is less interested in this kind of teaching. The provosts and deans who create more positions for adjuncts are themselves paid in the mid-six figures and have tenure.

So don't allow yourself to be exploited. Teach one class at a time as an adjunct when you feel like it, as some of the people profiled in this book do. It is usually a good experience, and it can give you credibility outside the institution. Teaching a subject can help you organize your own thinking about it. If you are independently wealthy or retired and already have a secure income, teach as many adjunct classes as you like. Theoretically, you are taking jobs away from potential tenure-track faculty, but that's their lookout. You didn't create the situation. What you should never do is to try to make your living this way. There are young academics who, frustrated in their efforts to land a tenure-track job, cobble together two or three adjunct jobs. They spend a lot of time commuting between campuses, never have any job security, earn very little, and have no time to work on original projects of their own. This kind of life does not lead to long-term employment. It is not living like a professor.

Why does this happen? United States Census data tells us there about 2.8 million people with Ph.D.s in the United States, 1.4 million of whom teach in institutions of higher education. Of those 1.4 million, half are part-time and not even a quarter have tenured or tenure-track positions. Even this proportion is declining. Plus, at any time, there are over a million graduate students in the pipeline. Clearly, the vast majority of these scholars are never going to obtain a tenure-track position at a university. Many of them would like to, because of the prestige and autonomy inherent in the job and because it allows them to live a life of intellectual inquiry. But universities simply overproduce Ph.D.'s. If every university professor had, on average, one graduate student who earns a Ph.D. in his or her entire career, then in a time of little growth in academia we would be in a steady-state situation. The true ratio of graduate students to professors is far higher than that—it is over six to one in biology, for instance. And the number of tenure-track jobs is going down, not up.

A widely discussed article in the *New York Times*, "Crowded Out of Ivory Tower, Adjuncts See a Life Less Lofty," calls attention to the plight of academia's one million low-wage workers. It profiles a recent Ph.D. in English who is teaching three or four classes a semester at the City University of New York for about $21,000 a year. He has no job security and no health benefits. He is forty-two years old, has a wife and child, and credit card debt. He can't save money or buy a home. The City University of New York alone employs over 10,000 other people like him! The article ends by saying that after eighteen months he has broadened his job search to include "positions at community colleges, or university presses, anything that would allow him to teach and pursue an intellectual life."

Indeed, the situation is so bad that there are Ph.D. support groups for the unemployed and underemployed. Another *New York Times* article, "The Repurposed Ph.D.: Finding Life After Academia—and Not Feeling Bad About It," describes such a gathering on New York's Upper West Side. The cult of academia has such a strong grip on the thinking of these otherwise mature and intelligent people that they need a great deal of support to even start to examine their non-university options.

What's it like to be a tenure-track college professor, supposing you can get the job? They don't really take summers off or have a lot of free time. Professors don't rank very highly on national surveys of job satisfaction, and it's easy to see why. To become a professor, you need to endure a long period of low pay and job insecurity both before and after earning your

Ph.D. You spend a decade (or two) with job titles like "graduate assistant," "post-doctoral fellow," "instructor," and "assistant professor." There are hundreds of qualified applicants for every tenure-track job, so the competition is intense. You have to work as hard as you can and as fast as you can to keep up. You can't allow yourself any self-doubt. You also have to be geographically flexible: If you get that job offer in Tennessee, you move there whether your family wants to go or not. Even after you get tenure, you still have to tolerate the petty demands on your time that are inherent in working for a complex and politicized institution. It's a little like joining a cult.

In return, you get a prestigious title, lots of autonomy, excellent job security (assuming you get tenure of course), decent pay, and most importantly you get to live in a world of ideas and intellectual inquiry. You get to be an expert on something. You work on projects of your own design that are interesting and even glamorous, at least to you, and you get to travel to conferences or to do fieldwork with somebody else paying for it. There's a lot to like about it, so no wonder hundreds of people apply for every opening. Professors, taken as a whole, may not have the greatest job satisfaction, but the more senior and successful professors are extremely satisfied. Many delay retirement as long as they can, and when they finally retire they often become an "emeritus" professor who has no responsibilities or pay, but still has the keys to an office on campus and a parking pass. How many other retired workers keep coming back to their old employer to work for free?

If you're reading this book, you're probably not a professor, but you may be a little wistful about having the good things that come with the job. You're a graduate student considering an academic career. You're an elementary or secondary school teacher and you recognize the similarity of your work to a professor's work. You are retired, or soon to be retired, and you are wondering what to do next. You're a stay-at-home parent and you are thinking about the years ahead. You're a young adult and it feels like the older generation took all of the interesting opportunities and jobs, leaving you nothing. Maybe you're a working professional who just wants something more. This book is really about how to enjoy the best parts of being a professor, without having to become one.

The thesis of this book is that you can take a normal, permanent job with benefits at a school, company, or government agency and still have the intellectual life you want. You don't have to sacrifice your dignity and your family's finances. As a public high school teacher, I earn five times what that City University of New York lecturer does, and I've probably published more academic papers in the last couple of years than he has too. High school teaching is still mostly done by full-time tenured or tenure-track teachers who receive a living wage and full benefits.

· ·

Profile: Sharon Barnett, naturalist

Sharon is one of the instructors at the Point Reyes National Seashore Association's Field Institute. She has bachelor and master degrees in environmental studies and education. Her primary job is at the Marin Country Day School where she works four days a week as a science specialist, developing and co-teaching science lessons with the regular classroom teachers. On one of her days off, she and I met over coffee so I could ask her about some of the other things she does in environmental education and natural history. Sharon is very active in these areas.

Like many young people, Sharon wasn't sure what to do when she graduated from college. Her first paid work after college was at the Beaver Lake Nature Center near her home in upstate New York. She showed up one day and offered to volunteer. She handed over her resume and the next minute the naturalist supervisor was saying, "Volunteer? Would you like a *job*?" One of their recent hires had just cancelled the day before, and they needed someone quickly. Sharon took over the position, living at the center and teaching classes for school groups and summer camps. From Beaver Lake, she moved to California and took a similar job at Walker Creek Ranch, where she worked several years as a "ranch naturalist," teaching environmental education for visiting school groups of 5th and 6th graders. Early in her career she took a course to become a Certified Interpretive Guide through the National Association for Interpretation. She feels the certification helped boost her career as a naturalist.

Sharon continued to volunteer in California. She was an elephant seal docent for the Point Reyes Natural Seashore, standing at a seal overlook spot in a red vest, educating visitors about the extreme life cycle of these amazing animals, and protecting the seals from the public during the breeding season. She did a short stint at the Marine Mammal Center, a wildlife rehabilitation facility, giving sick seals fish smoothies through feeding tubes on her first night there. She became one of the first creek naturalists for SPAWN, the Salmon Protection and Watershed Network, an organization which protects the endangered salmon and steelhead in Lagunitas Creek. She would lead walks along the creek during the fish-spawning season. She joined the board of directors of the Marin Audubon Society as the group's fundraiser. "I didn't have a lick of fundraising experience," she laughed. But she took a course on how to write grant proposals (Audubon paid for it) and won a few grants for the society. She no longer serves on the board but she still participates in the society's Christmas bird count every year.

Sharon also teaches classes and summer camps for pay on weekends and school breaks. She has taught summer camps on nature, wetlands, and birds at the Marin Art and Garden Center and the Richardson Bay Audubon Society Center and Sanctuary. She also taught summer camp at Wildcare, a wildlife rehabilitation facility with a small museum and a zoo for disabled animals and birds that can't be returned to the wild. She wasn't looking for that job. She just dropped by one day and, as at Beaver Lake, a camp teacher had just left and they were in dire need of a replacement.

Today Sharon regularly teaches Saturday community education hiking classes at College of Marin and natural history programs such as tide-pooling, birding, and nocturnal animals for families at the Point Reyes National Seashore. She has a number of adult students who take her hiking class again and again. Some of them said they wanted to go farther afield, so she organized an overnight trip to the Mendocino coast to see the natural history there. This was so successful that she organized another one to Lake Tahoe, and then a week-long natural history and hiking tour in Costa Rica. Now the group is planning an Alaskan trip. Sharon says, "It's a dream come true!" These trips are run through Marin Nature Adventures LLC, which Sharon founded with her husband Kevin Stockmann. They are guides for hire, taking clients out on natural history outings for half days and full days. Their clients are often family groups or birders visiting Northern California from somewhere else.

Recently Sharon was one of three co-founders, with Paola Bouley and Megan Isadore, of the River Otter Ecology Project, a citizen's science initiative. It includes a website, "Otter Spotter," where anybody can report river otter sightings in northern and central California, a number of "critter cameras" triggered by motion, and a scat DNA sampling program in collaboration with the California Academy of Sciences. River otters are making a comeback in our area, but very little is known about their populations and movements. The project's slogan is "Putting otters back on the map!" They now have an online map posting the specific details of hundreds of sightings. The projects attract donations, grants, and volunteers. There is a membership program and a wish list. Sharon threw herself into the project during the start-up phase, but it developed a momentum of its own and grew to be more than she could keep up with, given her other commitments. She is now an emeritus board member and loves searching for these charismatic animals during her outings. She continues to teach people about the otters' significance as an apex predator, and about the Otter Spotter program.

I asked Sharon about her travels. She is not a globe-trotter, but a friend at a travel company called High Country Passage did telephone her and say, "Would you like to go to the Galapagos?" So she served several times as a science teacher for the kids on a 90-passenger ship traveling among those islands. She has also taken field courses in Alaska and the Florida everglades, and has traveled to Nicaragua on a service learning trip with her school. She is thinking about future trips. She hasn't published much (yet), but she has some ideas for a children's nature book she may write some day.

A few years ago Sharon won the Terwilliger Environmental Education Award, our area's most prestigious award for teaching natural history. To put the award in context, Marin County has over a quarter of a million people, quite a few of whom are active in the community and passionate about the environment. The award often goes to an older adult in recognition of his or her life's work. It has been awarded posthumously. Sharon's family, friends, and co-workers wrote letters to the award committee in support of their nomination and she was chosen for it despite her relative youth. Sharon did not know they were doing this. "It was a huge honor and a huge surprise," she laughed. "Juan-Carlos (committee chair) called to tell me—I thought he was going to ask me to step in and teach a class."

On her motivation: "My real passion is to work with people and to learn more ecology. For me, it's not about recognition or money. A lot of people think that environmental education is just for youth. There's a need for it for adults as well. My reward—and this might sound silly but it is 100 percent true—when I walk away from a field experience with children or adults, I'm euphoric! It's like a drug—endorphins. Not 100 percent of the time, but maybe 90 percent. You see people make a connection to nature for the first time—it just floors me. Euphoric is the word. I feel really happy about that!"

6

Do Citizen Science

"There are no passengers on spaceship earth. We are all crew."
—Marshall McLuhan, quoted in *Paradigms Lost: Learning from Environmental Mistakes, Mishaps and Misdeeds* by Daniel Vallero

Sharon Barnett's River Otter Ecology Project is one example of many citizen science projects which are open to anyone to participate in. Citizen science projects aren't new. The Audubon Society's annual Christmas Bird Count has been running since the year 1900. It was originally started in response to traditional Christmas *hunts*, in which people would go out and shoot as many birds as they could whether they planned to eat them or not. In this survey project, you go out to a good spot for birding around Christmas, and under the supervision of a compiler you identify, count, and photograph birds according to a standard procedure. Your count is reported to the National Audubon Society. Your observations mean nothing by themselves, but they get combined with the results from tens of thousands of other volunteers around the country doing the same thing in the same year, and then the information is added to a data set that spans more than a century. That data set becomes a very powerful tool for studying and managing wild bird populations. All citizen science initiatives do essentially the same thing: recruit volunteers to make observations or measurements, standardize their procedures, and collect the results into one large data set. Digital communications have made all of this much easier, and have brought about a "golden age" for citizen science.

If you like studying birds at times other than Christmas, Cornell University's Laboratory of Ornithology has a number of citizen science programs. eBird, a joint project with the National Audubon Society, allows you to keep track of your own sightings and lists online, and to contribute your sightings to a real-time, globally accessible database. You can use the data to generate your own maps and graphs. Bill Schmoker, profiled in this book, participates in this project as a reviewer. In Project FeederWatch, you count birds at your own feeder, add your counts to the database, and see your data in the context of all the other thousands of feeders that have reported. For the NestWatch program, you find and monitor birds' nests, visiting them once every three or four days and reporting on the breeding success of the parent birds. There are online bird cams, free Adopt-a-School kits for teachers, an annual four-day "Great Backyard Bird Count" in February, just before the birds begin migrating north, and a program called the YardMap Network in which you map bird habitat in your area and work to improve it.

Birds lend themselves well to citizen science initiatives because they are everywhere and because of an established tradition of bird watching in the English-speaking world. Animals are more of a challenge, but there are citizen science projects for animals, too. Many, like the river otter project described earlier, involve reporting animal sightings in your area. A couple of professors in Chicago have one, Project Squirrel, in which you actually get to experiment on wild animals.

Project Squirrel has been operating since 1997. It is a joint project, sponsored by the University of Illinois and the Chicago Academy of Sciences. In its simplest form, you submit your observations of squirrels. After clicking on "Click here to record your squirrel observations," you are prompted to enter the date, time, and ZIP code of your observation and your own email address. You then enter the number of squirrels you saw, whether they were gray squirrels or fox squirrels, where you saw them, what kind of trees are there, what food they were getting, your gut-level impression of whether their numbers are going up or down, and the presence of dogs, cats, coyotes, and hawks in the neighborhood. In its more advanced form, you get to test squirrel bravery by building foraging patches (squirrel feeders), one in a "safe" site close to cover and a big tree and one in an "unsafe" open area. You use dried ears of corn and very meticulously weigh what gets eaten according to a specified procedure.

Gray squirrels and fox squirrels compete for territory and food. Their relative populations shift on a time scale of a few years. Project Squirrel's website has instructions on how to tell the two apart. Over the years they have learned that gray squirrels do well in Chicago's urban areas with parks and apartment buildings, but that fox squirrels prefer neighborhoods with single family homes. Gray squirrels need oak and pine trees to cache food (acorns and pine cones) but fox squirrels can get by with maples and elms. Fox squirrels also have a higher tolerance for dogs and cats.

People like this project because squirrels are engaging, and they are everywhere. There are lots of squirrel feeders in Chicago. Today, you don't have to live in the Chicago area to participate. The project's leaders even encourage you to submit observations from places without squirrels! It's still data. In fact, negative data can be quite important.

A project involving mammals with a smaller cute factor is the California Roadkill Observation System. A project with a much larger cute factor is the Barnard College/Columbia University Dog Cognition Lab's Project: Play with Your Dog.

There are plant projects too, like Project BudBurst, the California Phenology Project, and Nature's Notebook. "Phenology" is the study of seasonal changes in plants and animals, like the local dates for the first emergences of flowers, the first arrivals of migratory birds, or peak fall color in deciduous trees. As climate changes, so do these dates. Your observation of a nut dropping from a tree may not mean much by itself, but added to a big, long-term database it does mean something.

Two citizen science water quality programs that I have experience with are the New York State Department of Environmental Conservation's Citizens Statewide Lake Assessment Program (CSLAP) and the Stroud Water Research Center's Leaf Pack Network.

CSLAP, the New York State program, is over twenty-five years old. The state recruits individuals who live on or near a lake (and have a boat) to make periodic trips out into the middle of the lake to make some measurements and sample some surface water. These individuals are often members of a local lake association. You measure water temperature using a thermometer and water clarity using a device called a Secchi disk. The state provides all of the equipment except the boat. You also collect a sample of the water and filter a portion of it. You mail both the filtered water and the filter to a state lab, where they analyze its conductivity, pH, phosphorus, nitrogen, calcium, and chlorophyll. There is also the opportunity to get involved in special surveys for invasive plants and zebra mussels. I once served on the board of the Seneca Lake Pure Waters Association and participated in this program. Seneca Lake is so large that we had multiple sampling sites. At the time, we were the only lake association that sampled in more than one place and we felt a bit smug about that.

The Stroud Center's Leak Pack Network is a program for classroom teachers, although anybody can participate. The experiment you do is brilliant in the way that it combines stream ecosystem science with stewardship, biology with water quality. You purchase an inexpensive kit, which includes mesh bags, petri dishes and sorting trays, waterproof sorting sheets with illustrations of aquatic insects, thermometers, magnifying glasses and other utensils, and an instruction manual. You fill a mesh bag with dry local leaves and submerge it in a stream for several weeks. When you pull it out, you will find lots of aquatic invertebrates (mostly immature insects) hiding among the leaves. You sort and count: stoneflies here, mayflies there, caddis fly larvae in this dish, mosquito larvae in that dish and so on. Once you are done identifying, sorting, and counting there is a mathematical formula you can use to convert invertebrate counts into an index of stream water quality. This works because some species are much more tolerant of pollution than others. You enter your findings into a big database of course, but you also learn something right away about your specific stream that is worth knowing.

As with bird watching, astronomy has a long tradition of amateur involvement that continues today. The prominent comet hunter and writer David H. Levy is mostly self-taught, earning his university degrees in English literature. Dr. Levy has discovered or co-discovered about two dozen comets, including Shoemaker-Levy 9, the comet that collided with Jupiter in 1994. Of course, you have to live under dark skies or collaborate with a professional astronomer. David Levy does both. It's not by accident that he lives in Arizona. Today Levy earns money by speaking and writing about astronomy and he has built his own observatory, so perhaps you could call him a "professional amateur" astronomer. Two astronomical organizations with citizen science programs are the International Dark Sky Association and the American Association of Variable Star Observers. The National Aeronautics and Space Administration (NASA) and the Search for Extraterrestrial Intelligence (SETI) both have programs in which citizens can analyze some already-collected data on their home computers, looking for geological features on Mars (Be a Martian) or even for signs of intelligent life in the galaxy (setiQuest).

A national citizen science initiative with practical significance for everyone is San Francisco State University's Great Sunflower Project. Started in 2006 by biology professor Gretchen LeBuhn, the project's slogan is "Bees: responsible for every third bite of food." In fact, bees are responsible for almost all of the most nutritious foods that we eat. Grains like wheat and rice are wind-pollinated but most of our fruits, nuts, and vegetables require bees for pollination, and bee counts are declining in wild, agricultural, and urban areas. The pollination services from wild bees are worth literally billions of dollars to the agricultural industry.

In the original form of the project, you would be sent a packet of sunflower seeds (the annual variety "Lemon Queen") by San Francisco State. You would plant them in your yard. Once they flowered, you would record bee visits to the flowers according to a prescribed procedure. Lemon Queens are easy to grow, and bees love them. San Francisco State no longer mails packets of seeds to volunteers, and the project is no longer limited to sunflowers. Professor LeBuhn and her colleagues have expanded the protocol to include all flowering plants in all environments.

Data entry is through the project's website. You go to "Add a Count" and submit your observation. You can do a stationary count (quietly observe a single species of plant for 5–15 minutes) or a traveling count (while moving). You enter the species of plant, the estimated number of flowers, the date, start and end times, and the number of bees you saw. You indicate your location on a map. There are also options to submit area counts and even "casual observations," which have no time interval, distance, or area. Your bee counts get calculated as bees per hour per flower. A "My Data" page organizes your observations, locations, lists of pollinators, and your personal profile. There are bee observer cards to help identify bee species.

Today the Great Sunflower Project is a 501(c)(3) organization with 100,000 volunteers. It sponsors an Annual Great Bee Count every August. There is a really big data set and a nationwide map of observations. The data is shared upon request, but you can't easily look it up online without asking first. This is to protect the privacy of the volunteers.

How are citizen science projects relevant to your goals? Most experts have undergone periods of training in which they worked on somebody else's project. You might decide to do this to gain experience in a new field. It's one way to prepare your mind for creative ideas. As a volunteer for somebody else, you have an obligation to follow the project's procedures to the letter. The day will probably come when you think "these people aren't making the right measurements," which is another way of saying they aren't asking the right questions. You can suggest modifications of the procedure to the project's organizers. Before you know it, you might find that you are one of the organizers yourself. Or, you can use your experience to go off on your own. Maybe, like Sharon Barnett or Gretchen LeBuhn, you will identify an unmet need for data and start a citizen science project yourself.

· ·

Profile: Professor Gretchen LeBuhn

The founder of the Great Sunflower Project, Gretchen LeBuhn, is an ecologist and conservation biologist and a full professor at San Francisco State University. She earned her Ph.D. at the University of California at Santa Barbara. She always has several ongoing research projects. She gets grants to fund them, teaches biology classes, does fieldwork in the Sierras, publishes in scientific journals, writes books and chapters in books, instructs and advises graduate students, serves on committees and editorial boards, and gives seminars. All professors do things like these. Very few professors start big citizen science projects, though, and for that reason I wanted to interview her. A student of mine was interested in bees and wanted to meet her also, so Professor LeBuhn graciously met with the two of us and talked about how she conducts her studies and pursuits.

Gretchen is ambivalent about the role of honeybees in our lives. Keeping bees is a great way to connect with nature, she notes. Honeybees are necessary to agriculture. In North America, however, they are really domesticated animals that we have allowed to wander freely. Honeybees come from Europe. "They are invasive, nonnative animals that have escaped," she says. "They are smarter than chickens, in that they escape better." In agricultural areas, this is good, because they pollinate food plants. Gretchen is concerned about small wild areas on public lands being overrun by pet bees. She was trained in botany. She knows that the pollinator services provided by honeybees are not beneficial to native plants. It may even hurt them by facilitating the spread of nonnative plants. The native plants do fine being pollinated by native bees, which in turn establish quickly if there are plenty of native plants. We wouldn't want feral chickens running free in our nature preserves, but we allow it with honeybees.

The project began when Gretchen had a grant to look at pollinators in California's wine-producing Napa and Sonoma valleys. There was barely enough money to pay one graduate student to collect the data. The vineyard managers and workers Gretchen had already visited were always so helpful and interested in her research that she decided maybe she could just ask them to collect data. She planted sunflowers at the vineyards and handed out data sheets. The experience showed her that untrained observers could generate good data if they were properly prepared. (She initially asked them to count pollinator visits to flowers for an hour at a time—she had to modify that part of the procedure!) After that, she built the project's website and sent an email to fifteen or twenty master gardeners in southeastern states. Master gardeners are volunteers, usually affiliated with a land grant university's cooperative extension agent. They are experts on horticulture and provide advice, training, and service to the gardeners in their communities. They give presentations and write articles in local newspapers and newsletters, so Gretchen thought the master gardeners could help recruit some volunteers. She expected maybe a thousand sign-ups. She got 25,000 volunteers the first year. She had committed to send each volunteer a packet of Lemon Queen sunflower seeds. Needless to say, the postage strained her budget.

Like most citizen science websites, the Great Sunflower Project's site has to accept login information and record the data that volunteers enter. Gretchen had help building the site from a relative who is a professional computer programmer. They used Drupal, which is an open-source content management system, suitable for websites. Her relative still manages the site. He charges her a reduced rate.

I asked her about her findings. Gretchen compares her continent-wide data on pollinator visits to flowers with weather and precipitation data and maps of pesticide use provided by the U. S. Environmental Protection Agency and state agencies. She has found that where neonicotinoid pesticides are used, she sees a decline in pollinator visitation rates in the area. Neonicotinoid pesticides are new and their use is controversial. They affect the central nervous systems of insects. They may be a factor in colony collapse disorder, an incompletely understood trend affecting domesticated bees. Gretchen has plans to publish her findings in a major scientific journal.

The Great Sunflower Project gets data from all over North America. Gretchen is interested in extending it to other places, but she also has reservations about that. "Lemon Queen" variety sunflowers are still used by participants, but seeds of this variety are produced in the USA and cannot be shipped overseas. China would be a good place for the project ("There are pollution issues, and the Chinese love sunflowers") but she knows she would need a collaborator on the ground there to make it work. "Maybe Europe next year...," she muses. The truth is she already has a full-time job being a professor. This is not her only project, and she has always tried to keep the project the right size for her. This means not so expensive that she can't keep it alive for a year without funding, and not so time consuming that it prevents her from doing other things. Gretchen is the project's administrator. When a volunteer in Florida loses her password, Gretchen gets the email asking for help. "There are a lot of citizen science projects that start up and then die," she says.

Only 5 to 10 percent of the people who sign up actually submit observations. Spammers get in, and Gretchen and her colleagues have to meticulously validate the data. She curates it rigorously, and she is confident that her data set is absolutely clean. So although the volunteers aren't paid, citizen science data is not really free. "Free like puppies!" she laughs. "To have a successful citizen science project you have to give the participants something back. That means be responsive. Have a website that really works. It's a big job." On the positive side, she says it is gratifying to have public support. "When I started the Sunflower Project, I had no idea so many people would be willing to contribute."

. . . .

Profile: John Wade, Farallon Patrol skipper

Thirty miles west of the Golden Gate Bridge there are three sets of islands and islets called the Farallones. The word in Spanish means "pointy rocks sticking out of the sea." San Francisco's residents can see them on a clear day, but there aren't many clear days and hardly anybody goes there. That's because they are a national wildlife refuge, most of it federally designated wilderness. They are reserved for hundreds of thousands of seabirds, seals, and sea lions who need solid ground to rest on and raise their young. It's also because the sailing conditions between the bridge and the islands are so challenging. Twenty-five knot westerly winds are common. Tidal currents sweep in and out of the Golden Gate, interacting with the big swells that roll in from crossing thousands of miles of ocean. A notorious shallow spot outside the bridge, called the Potato Patch, throws up treacherous waves. It's always cold. Dense fogs form, and huge container ships pass in the fog. Most recreational sailors are content to cross under the bridge, turn around, and sail back into the bay.

There are always a few people on Southeast Farallon Island, though. With an area of one ninth of a square mile, it is almost spacious. An automated lighthouse sits on it and there is a research station staffed by scientists from Point Blue Conservation Science, a nonprofit organization. They study the birds and seals and other wildlife under a cooperative agreement with the United States Fish and Wildlife Service. Point Blue scientists have been on the island every day since April of 1968. This means they have a detailed and valuable long-term data set for the largest single seabird colony in the lower 48 states.

Situated on a bare rock, the station can produce nothing for itself except electricity from solar panels and a little rainwater. There is no room for a landing strip for airplanes. All of the food, fuel, supplies, and people have to come in by boat, and everything, including the waste the station produces, has to return to the mainland by boat. Point Blue cannot afford to keep a boat suitable for this work. Since 1971, the station has relied on the professionalism of volunteer boat owners who make regular runs to the Farallones and back to deliver people and supplies. There are about fifteen active Farallon Patrol skippers, and dozens more who have "retired." Every two weeks all year around somebody makes a run to the island.

This is a different sort of citizen science from the programs described above. Most citizen science programs get data from volunteers; the scientists can take the data or leave it. In this one, the volunteers provide essential logistical support in the field. It's very organized. There are rules and procedures, a commodore, a scheduling coordinator. Without the Farallon Patrol, year-around science would not get done on the Farallones. Intrigued by this, and because I love boats, I asked to come along on a run with veteran Farallon Patrol skipper John Wade on his 40-foot sailboat *Starbuck*. I knew that John and the *Starbuck* had made almost eighty runs to Southeast Farallon Island.

The marine weather forecast the night before was as good as it gets:

NW wind 10 to 14 kt. Clear. Mixed swell . . . NW 6ft at 9 seconds and SSW 1ft at 16 seconds. Wind waves around 1ft.

In fact, the winds were lighter than that and we had the boat's engine running much of the time.

The San Francisco Marina might be the most scenic place in the world to keep a boat. To the west is the Palace of Fine Arts, left over from the 1915 The Panama-Pacific International Exposition, the Golden Gate Bridge, and the Marin headlands. North across the bay you can see Alcatraz and Angel

Starbuck off Southeast Farallon Island. Photo by Michael Wing.

Island. Immediately to the east lies Fort Mason. Telegraph Hill and Coit Tower stand in the distance. Beyond them are the downtown skyscrapers, including the iconic Transamerica Pyramid. It's even prettier at 6:30 in the morning with the sun just coming up. A van with a Point Blue logo was being unloaded by a biologist and a volunteer. They had gone grocery shopping the night before, spending hundreds of dollars on food. They worked from a list that is organized aisle by aisle at the Safeway grocery store. Besides food, there were two full propane tanks, one full gasoline can, sealable buckets for bringing off compost, a water sampling kit, some personal mail, and one biologist with his personal gear. This is a light load for the Farallon Patrol.

We tied the fuel containers to the deck and put the food down below. Next John gave us the safety talk: I'm the captain; this is the man overboard procedure; watch for hypothermia; here are the radios and fire extinguishers.

The *Starbuck* has an outboard engine mounted on the transom, which is very unusual for a 40-foot sailboat. Most boats this size have inboard diesel engines. In fact, the *Starbuck* is unique. She was built in the 1970s by her first owner, Ralph Nobles, in his backyard. He started with a bare fiberglass hull made by a commercial boatyard, and added a deck, rigging, cabin, and everything else. She is a center-cockpit cutter, narrower and lower than most boats her size, which makes her light and fast to sail. I was told that when Ralph finished building the *Starbuck*, she had to be lifted over his house by a crane. She is named, of course, after the quiet, earnest, and decent first mate of the *Pequod* in Herman Melville's *Moby Dick*.

Besides the biologist, John, and me, there were several volunteer crew members and a Farallon Patrol skipper-in-training. Everyone is a bird lover or a sailor, and most of us are both. As we motorsailed out under the bridge, John told a story about an early run that Ralph Nobles had made before GPS was invented. They missed the island in the fog. They realized it when the biologists on board noted that passing seabirds were no longer flying ahead of the boat with fish in their bills—they were coming *towards* the boat with fish in their bills. Since the birds with fish were returning to their nests, the island must be that way. They turned around and found the island by smell. John says it's great to have biologists on board because they notice everything.

John gave me the wheel and I steered us past Point Bonita and through the Potato Patch, which was not scary at all on this mild day. We couldn't see the islands so we sailed with a compass heading of 240 degrees. The Golden Gate Bridge and California's coastline disappeared into the fog that was forming behind us. The Spanish fleet that sailed from the Philippines to Mexico in colonial times passed this way every year for 250 years without discovering San Francisco Bay. From this distance, it's easy to see why.

Common murres, Caspian terns, and elegant terns were all around. We passed a murre bobbing on the waves holding a large anchovy in his bill; a smaller bird stuck close to him. Mike, the biologist, explained that when they are a few weeks old, common murre chicks jump out of their nests and land on the water's surface. Sometimes they fall fifty feet. At that point they can swim but they cannot fly or fend for themselves. Their fathers jump in with them and for the next month or more the father and chick swim together on the ocean, father feeding the chick, until the chick learns to fly and catch food. The birds are small and the waves are big, so the two can get separated. Whenever this happens, the chick sets up a high-pitched squawking and the father squawks back in a grown-up murre voice. We heard this again and again as we sailed through the feeding areas and murres dived to escape us. We also saw a Northern fulmar. Mike said, "That's strange—that's a winter species."

Farther out we started to see shearwaters (Mike: "They tend to stay near the shelf break") and then a huge mola mola, or ocean sunfish. It lay pale and flat just under the surface of the water, looking like a fish that was run over by a steamroller. By lunchtime we could see the island, and we turned on the radio to tell them we were coming.

We hung fenders over our rail, but Southeast Farallon Island has no dock or pier. An aluminum and rigid foam vessel called a "SAFE Boat" came out to meet us, and attached a line to a giant mooring buoy that is anchored offshore. We tied up to the buoy using the line. Then the boat came alongside and tied up to us while we transferred our supplies. The boat motored toward shore where a big crane hung over the cliff. A hook on the crane was attached to a lifting bridle on the boat. Then, the crew on shore lifted the whole boat *with all of the gear and people still in it* fifty feet into the air. They placed the boat gently on land and the people got out. The process was repeated. John's crew usually gets a quick tour of the island before returning, and this was to be one of those days.

The island is steep and rocky. There are very few plants at this time of year except for an invasive weed called New Zealand spinach. Historic buildings house the scientists and their equipment. I could see from the water that the whole place is covered in bird poop. Birds are everywhere. The flat area where the scientists live is colonized by western gulls, with one nest every few feet in all directions. Since nesting season was almost over the gulls were just standing around and calling, each keeping to his or her space like campers in a campground. A few tufted puffins, my favorites, could be seen through binoculars on the cliffs. There is one northern gannet on the island, a lost visitor from the Atlantic Ocean.

On the way back, the biologist told us what it's like to live there. You can shower every four days. It's usually cold, damp, and windy but one day this week it was hot. People take turns cooking dinner. You can wash clothes, but then you hang them on a clothesline where a bird may poop on them. The rainwater they collect has bird poop in it too, so it has to go through an elaborate filtration and treatment process. When you pick up the baby birds to measure them, they poop or vomit on you. The outer clothing she wore on the trip home was smeared with bird poop, but she said she had changed into her last set of clean clothes underneath. Besides the biologist and her gear, we brought off two empty propane tanks, two empty gasoline tanks, a lot of empty food boxes, and some recycling, trash, and compost.

Why does John do this? "It's a guaranteed way for me to get some ocean time in," he says. Like many sailboat owners, he thinks about long-distance cruising but is too busy with work to take much time off. John works for conservation organizations, so there is some synergy with his day job. Also, the Farallon Patrol is a tradition that comes with the boat. His friend and colleague Ralph Nobles served on the Farallon Patrol before he sold the *Starbuck* to John, and John crewed for him then. John wants to continue that legacy. When you sail on the *Starbuck,* it feels like Ralph is an invisible member of the crew. His handiwork is all around you.

I love all kinds of boats and I am a boat owner myself so it's hard for me to say this, but a lot of people who have boats probably shouldn't have them. A lot of people who have big boats should have small boats. Most boats hardly ever get used. Where I live, the waterfront has billions of dollars' worth of impressive yachts sitting at their slips but most days the bay is empty. If you walk around to the back and sides of any marina building, you will see hundreds of derelict boats stored on land, quietly decaying.

I bring up this depressing fact only because the best solution to the "hardly-ever-used boat" syndrome isn't to sell the boat. It's to use the boat more often. Having a sense of purpose and a commitment to others helps. Once John signs up to do a Farallon Patrol run, he makes it his top priority. People are depending on him. Nothing but really bad weather will stand in the way. His service to Point Blue adds meaning and joy to his ownership of the *Starbuck* and gets him out on the water more often. On the runs, he meets interesting people he wouldn't meet otherwise and sees spectacular wildlife. He goes to a place that hardly anyone ever sees up close. All boat owners should be this fortunate. If you have a boat that you're not using enough maybe you should find some scientists in your area who need support, or find a program like New York State's CSLAP (described earlier in this chapter). If there isn't one, you could be the one to start it. John even thinks about extending his activities farther offshore: doing biological transects or whale studies in collaboration with the appropriate biologists and federal agencies.

7

Publish Your Work

"Let us guess that whenever we read a sentence & like it, we unconsciously store
it away in our model-chamber; & it goes, with the myriad of its fellows, to the
building, brick by brick, of the eventual edifice which we call our style."
—Mark Twain, quoted in *The Art of Authorship* by George Bainton

You should try to publish what you do and accomplish, partly for your
own satisfaction and for closure, partly to get credit for what you did,
but also for posterity so that future interested people can read about it and
won't have to repeat your work. Articles in peer-reviewed journals are the
gold standard among academics but there are also newspaper articles,
newsletters, books, web pages, and blogs. It's easier now than ever to get
the word out.

If you've never published a paper in a peer-reviewed academic journal,
you will find the process rigorous, but you don't have to be a professional
scholar to do it. Publishing your results in a journal may be appropriate if
you had to read articles in academic journals to learn the context for your
project, if you were able to (mostly) understand them, and if you think
your finding is just as important as what the articles you read have to say.
I've been the lead author on this process six times; each time the process
was basically the same.

The first step is to pick a journal. You can ask a professional for advice,
but usually the most appropriate journal is the one whose articles you
looked at most while doing the project. You should reread a few of the
articles from it to get the feel of what's expected, and the format they use. In
scientific journals, most articles contain the following parts: title, abstract,
introduction, materials and methods, results, discussion/conclusions,
acknowledgements, and references.

The title is not the place to get fanciful or self-indulgent. It needs to spell
out what you did in just a few words. A title expressed as a question some-

times works well. The abstract is a summary of the whole paper condensed into one long paragraph, but I always write this part of the paper last, not first. The same goes for the title. After the title, comes your name(s) and your institutional affiliation.

The place to start writing is the introduction section, where you explain the context for your work, and the rationale for why you did what you did, and what you hoped to find out. Here you have to refer to the past research done by others that you have read about. You cite the sources in the text according to your journal's preferred format. By the time the reader has finished this section, he or she should understand what the question is, what is already known about it, and why it matters.

The materials and methods section spells out what you did. The goal here is to give enough detail so that in principle any reader could do the same thing. The results section shows what you found, including text but probably also tables of numbers, graphs, maps, illustrations, and photographs. The discussion/conclusions section puts your results in the context of what was already done, and explains what it all means. It may also identify unresolved questions ripe for future research. The acknowledgements section thanks everybody who helped you, and the references section lists in alphabetical order, by author, the articles and books you cited in the text of your paper.

Once the manuscript of your paper is as good as you can make it, you send it off to the journal you selected. They will reply with a short communication saying they received it. Then many months will probably go by with no word. You will wonder if they have forgotten all about it. You need to understand that "peer-reviewed" means "reviewed by volunteer assistant professors who have no time." Your paper may take only thirty minutes to read, but it has to sit around in somebody's "in" box for a season or two first.

Eventually you will get a reply, with specific feedback. It will fall into one of three categories: (1) your paper is rejected, and here's why... (2) your paper will probably be accepted if you revise it: fix, change, add, or delete X, Y, and Z... (3) your paper is accepted as it is. (This last reply is rare unless you are very famous.) If revisions are called for, they could be as simple as rewording your conclusion or as involved as redoing some of your experiments. You try to give them the revisions they want, and send it in again. This part can be hard on your ego. Of the three reviewers of my stone line manuscript, one called it "excellent" and said to publish it as is, one dammed it with faint praise, and one was negative to the point of being nasty and belittling. All three reviewers were professional archaeologists with similar backgrounds and all three read the same document. It can definitely make you wonder if you have enemies you don't know about. (You rarely ever learn who the reviewers are; although they know who you are.) Fortunately in this case, the editor himself liked the paper better than two of the three reviewers, so it wasn't rejected out of hand.

Recently I was on the other side of this process. I got a message from the editor of the *New Zealand Journal of Forestry Science* (!) saying that some New Zealand scientists had written an article on spiral grain in pine trees there, and would I review it for them? I have never been to New Zealand or worked in a sawmill, but I guess my article on twistiness in bristlecone pines had made me one of the go-to experts in this admittedly small field. I was sent the manuscript with some detailed determinations to make: Is the question the paper poses new? Has it been well-defined? Are the methods the authors used appropriate, well-described, and replicable? Is the data properly reported? Do the figures look genuine and not improperly manipulated? Are the discussion and conclusions supported by the data? Does the title and abstract accurately communicate the paper's contents? Is the quality of writing acceptable? How important is this paper?

It had some unfamiliar looking mathematical equations in it. I had to read and reread this part and write down in plain English what each term and symbol meant. Once I had done that, I saw what the authors were trying to do. I don't love math, but too many smart people are unnecessarily afraid of it. Math is just counting.

I especially liked the way the editor broke the revisions into three categories. "Major compulsory revisions" are ones the authors will have to fix, or else the paper is rejected. If I as the reviewer demand these, a revised manuscript will be sent to me to read again and approve or reject. I didn't see a need for this. The paper was fundamentally sound; just improvable. "Discretionary revisions" are suggestions that the authors ought to consider and act on, but don't have to in order to get the paper accepted. I offered a number of these. "Minor essential revisions" are mechanical ones like mislabeled tables. The authors have to fix them, but can be trusted to do so without another review by me because they are no-brainers. There were a few of these, too.

How did the editor get my name? Most likely the authors had read my bristlecone pines paper and suggested me as a reviewer. I always suggest possible reviewers when submitting a paper to a journal; I never know whether or not they use my suggestions. I know that the New Zealand authors at least read my paper because they cited it in theirs.

None of the academic journals in which I have published charge the author anything, nor do they pay the author or reviewers anything. No money changes hands either way. The reputations of the journal and the author are both enhanced when the right article is placed in the right journal. The journal earns money from subscription fees and the author earns credibility, which can result in promotions, job offers, consulting gigs, or getting funded on future projects. The reviewer is usually a professor; he or she gains experience and influence in the field by doing the review. In my case, I just did it for the experience. It took me about six hours over several days. I didn't make anyone wait for months before I got started.

If you're a professional in the field, you already know which journals are legitimate. These days, there are a lot of fly-by-night "junk" academic journals that can look and sound the same as the real ones to most people. If you're brand new to the field, or not really in the field, you can get scammed. Here are the signs that a journal is legit: Experts mention it to you as a possible place to publish. You had to read a paper published in it in order to understand the background for your own project. The journal has been around for several decades. It publishes in hard copy, not just online. You can find it in a university library. It has picky editors, professors at major universities, who make you jump through all kinds of hoops to get published in it.

A "junk" journal usually is only a few years old. Nobody has heard of it. It may publish only online, and it will definitely ask you to pay to be published. If it gets your name somewhere, it will solicit you to publish. It will not reject your paper, or be overly picky about it. It's pointless to publish in one of these fake journals; nobody will read your paper and you will gain no credit or credibility from it. Since I've published in a few real journals, these fake ones are always spamming me. There are fake academic conferences too; perhaps because of my surname I am always getting email invitations to bogus conferences in China on subjects for which I am utterly unqualified.

Writing a book

Writing a book is also a possibility for big projects. Once you have an idea, an outline, and a chapter or two, you can approach a university press, a literary agent, or a commercial publishing company. You can also self-publish by engaging a printer to produce copies of the book for you. This will require some capital up front, and then it's up to you to store, market, and distribute the books they send you. Not all self-published books are money losers. My wife's elementary school teacher Ralph Shanks (profiled below) has made money on his seven critically acclaimed, beautiful, self-published books that are also meticulous works of scholarship. One of them has had eleven printings!

I never thought of writing a book before this one. The idea came to me when my sister-in-law Jennie Grant wrote a book, *City Goats*, about keeping pet goats in Seattle. She actually got the Seattle city council to change its laws about farm animals, and some newspaper articles were written about her. A publisher, Mountaineers Books, approached her and asked her to write the book, which she did. I thought that if a book could get published on such an arcane (although entertaining) subject then maybe I had a chance to publish one, too. The ideas for this book came to me in stages during a long drive down Interstate 5 from Seattle to San Francisco. I had nothing to write with; I tore a page out of a hotel telephone book to scribble notes on. By the time I arrived in the Bay Area, I had an outline.

Everyone writes differently. Even when I know exactly what I need to say, I can't do more than three or four hours at a stretch, or 1,000 words in a day. This book was written in bits and pieces that were smaller than that. I never blocked out big chunks of time for it and that's good because between my job, my family, and my projects I might never have started. I do go back over what I have already written obsessively, and I attempt to shorten and polish it. Other people work differently; when Jack Kerouac wrote *On the Road*, he spent three weeks typing the manuscript, with few breaks, onto a 120-foot roll of paper so he didn't have to pause to change sheets of paper. Truman Capote is supposed to have said, "That isn't writing at all, it's typing." So that's the other extreme. Of course, Kerouac had been living the life he wrote about, and keeping a notebook, for years before he sat down to his typewriter and roll of paper.

The largest publishers like Random House, HarperCollins, and Simon and Schuster don't accept unsolicited manuscripts. If you think your book has enough commercial value to be published by one of those companies, you need to get a literary agent to represent you. You pitch your book to the agent, and then the agent and you together pitch it to the publisher. That's what I did for this book.

I didn't know any agents when I started this process. I know one best-selling author who has one but I didn't feel comfortable asking him for a favor because his writing is so much better than mine. For a long time, I put off this difficult problem and focused on the more rewarding task of writing the book. But it's pointless to write a worthwhile book unless people are going to have a chance to read it. When the book was mostly done, I stopped working on it and started working on a book *proposal*.

Nonfiction books are sold to publishers on the basis of a proposal, not on the completed manuscript. The proposal itself can be dozens of pages long (mine was about 50 pages). The first page of my proposal had contact information, an estimated word count, a title, and a table of contents. The second page contained an executive summary that restated the rest of the proposal in glowing and confident language. I had to write the executive summary last of all. The self-promoting tone was difficult for a modest person like me to pull off.

The next section of the proposal was titled "Target Market." I wrote several pages on the demographics of the people who might be expected to buy this book: academics, K-12 teachers, retirees, etc. I cited specific numbers for each category of potential reader and evidence from newspaper articles for an unmet need for this kind of book. In the "Competitive Analysis" section I identified several other successful books that are similar to this one and discussed how they are similar and how they are different. You can't say, "No other book is anything like this." If that is true, agents and publishers will question whether there is a demand for it. You also can't write a book that is indistinguishable from dozens of already-published competitors. Business books and retirement books are particularly crowded fields this way. I was able to satisfy myself and my agent and publisher that this book is unique enough, and has enough general interest, to be commercially successful.

The next two sections of my proposal were the "Author Biography and Platform" and "Marketing and Promotion Plan." The word "platform" gets used a lot in the publishing world; it means anything you do that will help sell books. Examples include speaking at the meetings of professional organizations and writing for their newsletters, having a blog with followers or a website with lots of visitors, previous books, media exposure, lots of friends, etc. The marketing and promotion plan outlines how you will leverage these relationships and activities to get a lot of attention for your book when it is released. Publishers today don't do that much to promote the books they publish. They expect the author will do it. After these sections came my chapter outline, which was not so different from that scribbled-on page from the hotel telephone book that got me started. I described each chapter and each profile in two or three lines. Following that was about twenty pages from the manuscript.

Now that I had a proposal to sell the book, I had to write a query letter to sell the proposal. Nobody is going to read fifty pages without a good reason. The query letter is a one-page cover letter to an agent, explaining why the book is sure-fire guaranteed to be a success. The text of the query letter I used is attached to the end of this book as an appendix. But, who should I send the letter to?

I found a list of major literary agencies, most of which are in New York. I went down the list and studied the website of each agency. You are not supposed to query more than one agent at each agency. There must be no economy of scale for literary agencies, because there are lots of them and they are all pretty small. Like law firms, they have similar sounding names. Many have only half a dozen agents, or fewer. As an outsider in this business, I found it strange that agents don't specialize by genre more than they do. Most agents represent both fiction and nonfiction. It's pretty common to find one individual who does children's books, literary fiction, memoir, self-help, romance, Christian books, cookbooks... If almost all agents represent almost all genres, how should I select the ones to approach? I had to carefully read the online biographies of each agent at each agency to find out what kind of books she or he represents and what each one likes to read. For each agency, I selected one agent that seemed the best fit. Often the deciding factor was just instinct.

Once I selected a particular agent at a particular agency, I had to customize my query letter to meet that agent's preferences and submission requirements. Most agents prefer email, but a few prefer snail mail. Some just want a query letter, some a letter and a short writing sample, some a letter and a full proposal. Some want the proposal or writing sample as an attachment; many insist on its being pasted into the body of the email. Some agencies have their own online submission forms. There were forty agencies on my list and I worked my way down it a few at a time, researching and selecting agents and sending query letters. I discovered sixteen of them to be not appropriate for my project. They only did children's books, or Christian books, or fiction, or they weren't taking on new authors or something like that. I didn't bother these agencies with my query letter. Of the twenty four I did query, sixteen of them never replied. Five said "No" with response times varying from a few hours to several months. Three asked for more information, and I signed a representation agreement with one of these about a month after starting the process.

Now that I had an agent at a respected agency, I resolved to follow her lead. I sent her what she asked for, trusted her advice, and I tried not to be a pest. I understood that courtesy, patience, and professionalism go a long way in publishing, as in any business. Literary agents aren't paid anything until they sell your book to a publisher. Even after they do, it's not a huge amount of money. So I waited. She helped me revise my proposal and she sent it out to publishers. I waited some more. At intervals I offered her suggestions for publishers that seemed like a good fit, even including the names of individual editors at those publishers. Nothing happened. After a longer time than I care to admit, I broke up with her (amicably).

What went wrong? Agents really can't afford to promote your book like you can. Remember, they are paid nothing until it sells. When it didn't get snapped up quickly by a major publisher, my agent must have realized she was throwing good hours after bad. She probably became discouraged and put it on the back burner. It's a quirky book by an unknown author. Publishers don't always know what they want, or what their customers will want. When J. R. R. Tolkien finished *The Lord of the Rings*, it took him five years to get it published even though he had already made a big commercial success with *The Hobbit*. *The Lord of the Rings* became the best-selling novel ever written. Tolkien could afford to spend years dickering with difficult publishers and editors because he had an emotional investment in the book he had written. So could I; my agent couldn't afford to do that. So I went with plan "B" and contacted some publishers directly. This book is the result. I was very encouraged by the fact that even though my agent didn't actually sell the book, she had believed that she could.

To an outsider, all of this seems rather wasteful of people's time. Agents (and smaller publishers) have to wade through thousands of unsolicited submissions looking for the few that appeal to them, and authors have to query a lot of agents and/or publishers, who are paid nothing to read queries, until a match gets made. This industry is changing rapidly and trade books are becoming less profitable on average even while more of them are being published. Probably some new system will emerge in the years to come, but almost nobody is predicting the end of books. There will always have to be some sort of vetting process.

Another option is to approach a university press. You don't need an agent to do that. They publish on scholarly subjects and they aren't as concerned about how many copies your book will sell as for-profit publishers are. Harvard University Press, the University of Chicago Press, University of California Press, and the University Press of New England are examples, but there are over a hundred others. If your book is on some local or regional topic, a local or regional university press is the most likely to be interested. Pitching your book to a university press is like pitching to an agent; you use a query letter and a proposal. I learned about agencies, query letters, and book proposals by studying agencies' websites and agent's blogs. A book edited by Robert Lee Brewer called *Writer's Market*, published annually, was also helpful.

Amazon.com's Kindle Direct Publishing program allows you to offer your book for sale as an e-book for Kindle electronic devices and applications. You create an account with Amazon and prepare the electronic file to conform to their requirements. There is plenty of guidance and lots of tools on Amazon's website to help with this. It looks easy, and there is almost no barrier to entry. The question is whether you want to publish in a place that that has no barrier to entry. You upload your file, preview it, confirm that you have the publishing rights, select from a range of pricing and royalty options, and click "submit." It goes for sale online. You can actually earn more money per book than if you publish the traditional way. You can change and update your e-book even after publishing it. There are marketing and promotional tools you can employ. Electronic publishing is an evolving field; the details change rapidly.

Something about writing a book that took me by surprise was copyright issues. If you are writing a school paper or blogging on a website, it is pretty common to take an excerpt from somebody else's published work in order to comment on it or illustrate a point. The epigrams at the beginning of these chapters are examples. But when you publish a book, you can't re-use somebody else's words, even properly attributed, without getting permission. That can be a cumbersome process, neither quick nor cheap. If you're wondering why so many of the epigrams and quotes in this book are from before the 20th century (and why so few women are quoted), that's the reason. Anything first published before 1923 is in the public domain: fair game. Very little that was published after 1923 is. There were some quotes and excerpts from Emily Dickinson, Robert Frost, Maria Montessori, T.S. Eliot, and Martha Graham that I wanted to use. They're all over the internet. But getting formal permission wasn't worth it. There is a doctrine of "fair use" that appears to permit the use of extremely short excerpts (something like ten words) without obtaining permission, but it's a legal gray area.

The magazines and newsletters of nonprofits and professional organizations are easier to get published in than academic journals and they also get the word out to the people who care, so you should consider that option. Examples of this are William Motzer's articles in *Hydrovisions* and *The Vortex*. You can pitch your article or idea to the editor, or sometimes the editor will come to you. For example, I submitted an abstract to the American Chemical Society's national meeting on the subject of this book. As a result, they contacted me and asked me to write an article for their magazine *Graduate & Postdoctoral Chemist*. I sent them a 1,200-word piece titled "Get a Regular Job and Live like a Professor." This was seen (and read, I hope) by 20,000 people. I may "reslant" this article for some other professional societies that I belong to, like the American Geophysical Union.

Profile: Ralph C. Shanks, anthropologist

When my wife was in elementary school, she had a social studies teacher who was an expert on lighthouses and was writing a book about them. He would tell his students stories about lighthouses, and years later she remembered how cool it was to have a teacher who was a genuine expert on something interesting. Ralph Shanks still lives nearby, and I invited myself over to ask him about his projects. How do you go from third grade teacher to expert author?

Ralph earned his bachelor's degree from the University of California at Berkeley, and his master's degree in anthropology from San Francisco State University. Even though he was enrolled at San Francisco State, he worked with an anthropology professor he knew from Berkeley, the late Professor Larry Dawson. This grew into a long collaboration on California Indian baskets. Ralph says: "He was the best scholar in the world on Indian basketry, but he didn't like to write." Ralph does like to write. He was accepted into the University of Pennsylvania's Ph.D. program in anthropology, but decided he didn't want to leave California. Anyway the job market for professors was getting tight, even then. He got teaching credentials and taught elementary and middle school in San Rafael, California, for over 30 years.

Ralph is a recognized expert on California lighthouses and lifeboat stations, as well as on Indian baskets. His maritime history projects began when he got to know a lighthouse keeper and his wife (family friends) and wrote a book to preserve their stories. He feared they would be lost. "They were not going to get published any other way." He eventually wrote three books about lighthouses. *Guardians of the Golden Gate: Lighthouses and Lifeboat Stations of San Francisco Bay* is a popular favorite, and can be purchased at almost any lighthouse gift shop, historical society, or park visitor center on the coast. His book *The U.S. Life-Saving Service: Heroes, Rescues and Architecture of the Early Coast Guard* is assigned reading for the cadets at the U. S. Coast Guard Academy. Both of these books were edited by his wife, Lisa Woo Shanks.

Today, he is even better known for his work on baskets, especially for his books *Indian Baskets of Central California: Art, Culture, and History (Indian Baskets of California and Oregon, Vol. I)* and *California Indian Baskets: San Diego to Santa Barbara and Beyond to the San Joaquin Valley, Mountains and Deserts (Indian Baskets of California and Oregon, Vol. II)*, both also edited by Lisa.

To understand how important these books are, you have to understand the centrality of baskets to the traditional cultures of California Indians, and to California Indians today. Baskets were used for the storage and transportation of almost everything, and they had other uses that we today don't typically associate with baskets, like cooking, food processing, child care, and fishing. They were also given as gifts on important occasions, and frequently they had symbolic value. They were often decorated with feathers, beads, or shells. California had dozens of different Indian nations, speaking languages from a number of unrelated language families. There was more linguistic diversity here than any place in the world, except for the highlands of New Guinea. Each nation was divided into sedentary and territorial groups of sometimes just a few hundred people. Each group had its own techniques and traditions for making baskets, and each group used fibers from many different plants. There was much variety in basketry and the standards for craftsmanship were extraordinarily high, as they still are.

Ralph's books are full of photographs of stunningly beautiful baskets. They are organized by nation: Ohlone, Esselen, Pomo, Patwin, Coast Miwok, Wappo, etc. They're not coffee-table books, but works of scholarship. He takes a scientific approach to his discussions of the different materials, weaves, styles, and uses. He cites hundreds of other scholarly books and articles about baskets. His books will be read as long as there are people on earth who care about Indian baskets and cultures.

Ralph is an officer of the Miwok Archaeological Preserve of Marin (MAPOM), a nonprofit organization devoted to promoting accurate knowledge about the California Indian groups. His MAPOM affiliation is what opened doors with museums. Today, of course, his books do that also. He did his master's degree work at the Phoebe Hearst Museum of Anthropology at the University of California, so that is another affiliation that helped. He got some donations from Indian nations to work on some of his later books, but his work has been mostly self-financed.

Ralph has self-published all seven of his books. He created a company called Costaño books. The University of Washington Press helps distribute his series on Indian baskets, but they don't publish them. Early in his career he sent a manuscript of one of his lighthouse books to Stanford University Press, which rejected it because they said their priority was to publish the work of professors, although they acknowledged in their rejection letter that his writing was better than that of most Stanford professors! On self-publishing, Ralph remarks: "It's a risk. Publishing books is not cheap. You have to work to keep the books moving." Because of their subjects, many of his books are sold in museum and historical society bookstores, National Park visitor's center gift shops, and independent booksellers. He made a lot of sales calls. Today they are also available through Amazon.com and Barnes and Noble. Ralph has also published a few articles in academic journals, but prefers to write books.

To do his research, Ralph had to travel a lot. Many notable baskets are not located in California today. He has visited over fifty museum collections, some of them in the capitals of Europe. He and his wife Lisa worked with tribal offices all over North America while he wrote his book *North American Indian Travel Guide*. He has traveled up and down the California coast repeatedly in his research on lighthouses and lifeboat stations. Much of this travel was self-financed, doubling as family vacations. However, proceeds from his books have paid for his travel expenses after the fact.

I asked him if he had any advice for his younger self. He gave a wry smile and said, "You have to have a spouse that has a good job!" (She does.) He also remarked that if you are a teacher you need a good rapport with your administration. He taught part-time some years to free up time for writing.

Now retired from the San Rafael schools, Ralph teaches courses in the anthropology department at the University of California at Davis, at both the undergraduate and graduate levels. He has taught every age group from kindergarten to graduate school! He isn't technically a "professor" at Davis (he has no Ph.D., so his appointment at Davis doesn't use that term), but to his colleagues and students he is one of the world's foremost academic experts on California Indian basketry. He is working on the next book in his series on baskets. "I've had these really deep interests all my life," he says.

After I wrote this book and went through the process described above involving query letters, a book proposal, an agent, and a publisher, I had a new respect for what Ralph has done on his own. He was the first person I interviewed for this book; I called him back to ask for more specifics on self-publishing. For example, what exactly does it mean to "create your own company?" I asked. He said it was easy. He had to take out an advertisement in a local newspaper announcing it. He had to ask for a taxpayer identification number from the California Franchise Tax Board. He said he learned how to do it (and a lot of other self-publishing steps) in *Dan Poynter's Self-Publishing Manual*. You really don't have to create your own company to publish a book, though. If you have a social security number, you can do it as an individual. Your liabilities are not likely to exceed the capital you spend on the project if you're your own investor, and liabilities are the main reason for starting a company. Dan Poynter's book also took Ralph through the process of applying for a Library of Congress Control Number and an ISBN (International Standard Book Number).

OK, I said, so you have a company, a manuscript, some money, and those numbers; now what? Ralph's books on Indian baskets also have great photographs. He and his wife took most of them. They hauled their own professional camera equipment into the museum collections they visited; often they provided their own lighting. Their photos are so well done that museum curators would ask for copies. Ralph did not do his own layout or cover design on these books. He hired a professional designer named Jacci Summers. There was a lot of back-and-forth collaboration. Once the book was designed to his satisfaction, he hired Global Interprint, Inc. to produce a few thousand copies. The book was printed in Hong Kong. Once again, there were lots of back-and-forth communications, especially about image quality. Photographs of baskets need to show minute detail.

A moment would arrive when a large truck pulls up in front of Ralph's garage. Ralph has learned the hard way that some delivery companies will actually put the pallets of books *in* the garage; some will drop them off on the driveway. Ralph prefers the ones that put the books in the garage. Ralph would now own a garage full of books written by himself and be in the hole for thousands of dollars. He would have to sell books. Because of their regional subject matter, Ralph always has a pretty good idea of where his books can be sold. He made sales calls, either in person or by the U.S. mail and phone calls. He visited independent booksellers and asked to speak with the manager. He sent free copies to National Park Service visitor center bookstores. Usually they would order more. Bit by bit, the garage would empty. Ralph has gone through this many times. Recalling the first time, Ralph says, "I printed 2,000 copies of *Lighthouses of San Francisco Bay*. When they arrived, I didn't know if I would sell any." In addition to being a hardworking and talented writer, Ralph is just braver than most of us.

For his latest books Ralph approached the University of Washington Press for help with distribution. Ralph still publishes the books; the University of Washington does nothing until the books are printed. They list Ralph's books in their catalog and manage them online, a job Ralph prefers not to do himself.

. . . .

Poets have always been Hackademics

One difference between scientists and artists is that most scientists believe they need lots of resources (a job, an advanced degree, a laboratory, a grant, equipment and supplies, assistants) to be successful. Think of Charles Darwin, who had a university education (Edinburgh and Cambridge), the social status of a nineteenth-century English gentleman, family wealth, and a survey ship and crew courtesy of the Royal Navy to take him on a five-year tour of the southern hemisphere. Considering these circumstances, the fact that Darwin wasn't actually paid for his work (officially he was a "supernumerary passenger") hardly mattered. In contrast, artists understand they aren't going to get access to resources until after they've succeeded. Artists go ahead with what they have.

I wrote this book looking for people doing creative projects; people who leverage their affiliations and collaborations, apply for things, travel with purpose, teach, and publish. College professors do these things; so do poets. They have to! No other human activity pays so little or receives so little institutional support. Most mainstream publishers won't touch poetry. Even the United States poet laurate receives a stipend of $35,000 per year, less than a first-year kindergarten teacher in most school districts. (Past United States poet laureates have included Robert Frost, Gwendolyn Brooks, and Joseph Brodsky.) So poets hustle. They teach in prisons, nursing homes, schools, summer camps, writer's workshops, adult education programs, and after-school programs. They publish each other's stuff in anthologies and employ a publishing medium that's almost unique to poetry: the chapbook. A chapbook is a small and inexpensively produced paperback less than 40 pages in length and bound with a saddle stitch. They generally have day jobs: teacher, librarian, counseling psychologist, editor, or lawyer. A few poets are college professors, but the rest were hackademics way before anyone else.

The career trajectory of Kay Ryan, the sixteenth United States poet laureate, is a case in point. Ryan taught remedial English, part-time, at the community college down the street from my house. For decades. They didn't have her teaching college-level composition or creative writing, because there were tenured professors available to do that. Very few of her students or colleagues knew that she wrote poetry. Hailed as an "outsider poet," late in her life she won a Guggenheim Fellowship, the Ruth Lilly Poetry Prize, a MacArthur Fellowship, a Pulitzer Prize, and the National Humanities Medal. "Outsider poet" indeed! But you have to remember she was practically unknown until she was sixty.

Where I live there is a program called California Poets in the Schools (CPITS). Published poets who are active writers and have some teaching experience apply to become "Poet-Teachers." Once accepted into the program, they become independent contractors for CPITS, who can arrange to lead poetry writing workshops in schools, visiting the classroom of a regular teacher. They are paid for their time, typically $75–90 an hour. CRITS also produces anthologies of student poetry and organizes a performance program called Poetry Out Loud. It is the oldest such organization in the country, and one of the largest. My area has a long history of great poets. The beat poet Kenneth Rexroth had an illegal cabin near my school in what is today the Samuel P. Taylor State Park. Now state park archaeologists are studying the site of the cabin! It's funny how quickly the personal becomes part of history. But Rexroth was the emcee on the night that Allen Ginsberg read *Howl* to a shouting audience in San Francisco while Jack Kerouac passed the wine and Lawrence Ferlinghetti listened and decided to publish it. Gary Snyder lived in my school district too. Even Robert Frost spent the first decade of his life in San Francisco. CPITS poets sometimes come to my school, so I invited myself to talk to one.

· ·

Profile: Prartho Sereno, poet laureate

Have projects, affiliate, apply for things, travel, teach, and publish? Prartho Sereno has done all of these multiple times, and in multiple ways. She said yes to an interview right away when I explained why I wanted to talk with her. "I am definitely a hackademic!" she replied. She has been a California Poet in the Schools for eighteen years. We met in a coffee shop, with my teenage daughter coming along also to meet the poet. I've done interviews at peoples' homes and workplaces and even on boats, but half of them have been in coffee shops. Everyone feels comfortable in a coffee shop.

Sereno is intuitive, happy, intelligent, and absolutely a mystic. Early on she confessed to us, "My SATs were way higher in math than in English. I'm dyslexic." It surprised us to hear that a published writer would be dyslexic, so we asked what that's like. "You see round," she explained, "so the flat page is hard. But I'm attracted to the space on the page. Poetry is space, with words that help you see the space. Poetry helps you accentuate the silence without disturbing it." Prartho has led a peripatetic life as a mother, bartender, meditation instructor in Cornell University's physical education department, cook, family therapist, taxi driver, palm reader, and poet. Palm reading was one of the most remunerative jobs she has had. "It's been a less-than-direct-route," she admitted. Our interview was less-than-direct as well, veering all over the events of her busy life. Prartho aspires to be a "tour guide of the possible," a phrase that seemed especially apt to us in the context of this book. It's reminiscent of Abraham Maslow and the human potential movement of the 1960s, and also of Emily Dickinson's poem "I well in Possibility." Prartho says, "The best poem you can write is the poem that *only you* can write. That's what I tell my students at all levels."

Her creative projects include poems, books, and paintings. Like Ralph Shanks (profiled earlier), she has created her own small press to publish one of her books but unlike him she has published books through traditional publishers also. She has also published individual poems in a number of literary reviews. Her five books are titled *Everyday Miracles: An A to Z Guide to the Simple Wonders of Life* (Kensington Publishing), the chapbook *Garden Sutra* (Finishing Line Press), *Causing a Stir: The Secret Lives & Loves of Kitchen Utensils* (illustrated by herself and self-published by Mansarovar Press), *Call from Paris* (The Word Works), and *Elephant Raga* (Lynx House Press).

Prartho is good at applying for things and getting grants and awards. She enters contests as a route to getting published: *Elephant Raga* won the 2014 Blue Lynx Poetry Contest (with a $2,000 prize) and *Call from Paris* won The Word Works Washington Prize. Even her self-published *Causing a Stir* won a bronze IPPY (Independent Publisher Book Award). She published it herself because she had previously signed a contract for it with a publisher and then the publisher went out of business. Her daughter professionally designed it for her. She obtained a Library of Congress number and an ISBN for it, a process described earlier in this chapter. "It was my greatest success and my greatest failure," she sighed, "but I pulled it off." The book eventually sold about 2,000 copies. She has been nominated for a Pushcart Prize, one of America's most recognized literary awards. One year she won the Radio Disney Super Teacher award for her work as a California Poet in the Schools. She was nominated by a student for it. She has also received a Marin Arts Council Individual Artist grant. But although she started writing as soon as she was old enough to read, she didn't really start submitting her work until she was over forty. She made a deal with some literary friends then that the first person to accumulate 100 rejections from publishers would be taken out to dinner by the others. She won that dinner, but got published too. Her Washington Prize from The Word Works came to her on her third try. First she was a runner-up, than a finalist, then she won it.

So how does one get to be Marin County poet laureate? The award was founded and funded by a private individual and then taken over by the Marin Free Library System. The committee has its eye on people and somebody nominates you. You get invited to submit a proposal for the outreach activities you will do if you get the award. They interview three finalists, looking for solid creative work and contributions to the community. As poet laureate, Prartho works with the Marin Poetry Center (where she was on the board of directors and was the high school poetry coordinator) to organize high school "arts mashups": students at one school write poems while students at another make paintings. They send each other their work and then make new works that respond to what they have been sent. Then everything gets exhibited to the public at an off-campus venue, the Falkirk Cultural Center. "It's art speaking to art," she explains.

Prartho has made ten trips to India over three decades, each up to six months in duration, and totaling about four years there. She lived in a bamboo hut at an ashram. "That's why I couldn't have a normal job," she explains. "I have a huge love affair with India. When I return there—when I arrive and I smell the air, I'm home! Even just saying that I feel relaxed; my shoulders drop. There's timelessness there. There's deep space there—the vast interior space. Even the beggars make jokes out of nothing. [She tells a story from one of her poems about a fruit vendor loudly singing the praises of the diverse and delicious fruits he has to sell. All that's actually in his basket are a few lemons.] You enter your senses like you've never been there before. I was always very physical. The body doesn't lie." Prartho's master's thesis in psychology was about the relationship between creativity and sensory awareness.

She also does book tours. She went to twenty-three cities for *Everyday Miracles*. "Always on my own funds," she says. She arranged her own travel, staying with friends. She has lived in so many different places—Ohio, California (both northern and southern), New York, Indiana, and Oregon, among others—that she can often claim local status. She called up bookstores and (in the case of *Causing a Stir*) kitchen supply stores. They usually said "Yes"—they want writers to come. She read selections of her work and afterwards sold some books.

At College of Marin she teaches an adult education course called The Poetic Pilgrimage: Poem-Making as a Spiritual Practice. "Again, on the fringe…" She smiles, and continues, "It's not a religious class. The word spirit comes from breath anyway; it means you're alive. Almost all the men who take it are retired physicians." On teaching at juvenile hall: "I bring Mary Oliver to juvenile hall. Everyone else brings rappers. We have a rule that we are not there to celebrate anything that brings you here—no drugs, violence, or illegal activity." (Mary Oliver is a Pulitzer Prize-winning poet whose work could be described as poignant, passionate, and very much about nature and solitude.)

Prartho earned an MFA (Master of Fine Arts) degree in creative writing from Syracuse University when she was over sixty. This was no part-time extension school gig or online program. She went off to graduate school the same way a 22-year-old would. She applied to a couple of universities and Syracuse awarded her a teaching assistantship that covered her tuition and fees and paid a stipend. She couldn't have afforded it otherwise. Prartho has never been wealthy. For most of three years she lived at Syracuse, returning to her California home in between semesters. We asked her why she did it. "I wanted to do this; maybe get an academic job", she said, "but the main reason was to have time to write. I was really busy being a Poet in the Schools." At one point, she had been visiting 75 classrooms a year in the schools. An MFA in creative writing is considered a "terminal" degree. That means that it's the highest academic degree possible; there is no such thing as a PhD in creative writing. An MFA qualifies you to teach writing at the university level, but an academic job eluded her. For a moment Prartho looks a bit wistful about not having the regular paycheck and benefits that would come with that, but she is too positive to dwell on it. "My writing was a little too joyful for them! They trusted pain, suffering, sorrow. But joy can be honest too."

Maybe poetry is not so different from science or history or anthropology. Don't they all consist of looking at something more closely than anyone else, and saying to the rest of the world "look at this"? Poets get to make things up and scientists are not supposed to do that, but the creative impulse must come from the same place. So we probably all have things to learn from poets about being resourceful with what we already have.

8

Achieve Creative Flow

... we must rather class happiness as an activity, as we have said before, and if some activities are necessary, and desirable for the sake of something else, while others are so in themselves, evidently happiness must be placed among those desirable in themselves, not among those desirable for the sake of something else; for happiness does not lack anything, but is self-sufficient.
—Aristotle, *Nicomachean Ethics*, Book X, Chapter 6, translated by W. D. Ross

This book is about how real people have obtained satisfaction and success by doing specific achievable things, and how others can do the same. I'm no life coach or self-help guru, and it's at the risk of losing my reader's trust that I examine this subject at all. However, psychological research does have something to tell us about what works to make us happy and what doesn't. It is well supported by this research that having creative and original projects to do, which are both enjoyable and challenging and can lead to modest, earned, personal success, promotes happiness. There's even evidence that having a sense of purpose may add years to your life. You'll need extra years to bring your projects to fruition. Because of that, I am going to examine this subject. Doesn't everyone want to be happy?

For the individual, asking, "Am I happy?" has been compared to looking for your shadow with a flashlight. The question resets your mood to neutral. We also delude ourselves that we are wiser than those around us. Even though everybody agrees that once basic needs are met more money doesn't make people happier, we plan our lives as if we were the exception and try to get more money. We are not very good at dealing with this question, which is why we're lucky to have experts who use the scientific method. What follows is a summary of the work of several authorities on the subject of happiness, including Mihaly Csikszentmihalyi, Tal Ben-Shahar, Barry Schwartz, Martin Seligman, Philip Brickman, and Abraham Maslow.

Let's first examine what happiness isn't. It isn't getting whatever you want. In fact, getting everything you want can unhinge you. One has only to look at the public lives of our richest, most famous, and best loved celebrities to see that. Sports stars and entertainers do bizarre and self-defeating things to themselves at the heights of their fame. They even kill themselves. Do they hate themselves for being great? Maybe their success feels unearned to them, or at least disproportionate. Happiness also doesn't come from having infinite opportunities. Barry Schwartz, who studies this question, calls it "the paradox of choice." Too many options cause anxiety, especially for the personality type Schwartz calls the "maximizer," which is someone who has to be certain that each choice made is the best possible one. In the modern world this is hard to do.

Hedonism—the proverbial sex, drugs and rock & roll—doesn't promote happiness either, as anyone who has tried that life for any length of time can tell you. Surprisingly, even luck has little effect on your long-term happiness. Philip Brickman and several co-workers did a famous study comparing people who won the lottery with a control group who didn't and a third group of accident victims who were paraplegics. They found that the positive effect on happiness of winning the lottery wore off quickly, as did the negative effect of losing the use of your legs! From this result, they conceived the "set-point" theory of happiness: External events make little long-term difference. Whatever happens, your mood soon returns to your individual hard-wired "set-point," which is genetic.

Does that mean nothing matters to happiness? It does not, because winning the lottery or having an accident is just luck. There's lots of evidence that *work*, and the resulting fruits of one's labors, have more durable and lasting effects on happiness. The Hungarian-American psychologist Mihaly Csikszentmihalyi has spent his life studying happiness and creativity. He has identified a state he calls "flow." When you're in a state of creative flow, you are completely absorbed in the task at hand and you are doing it for its own sake, not for an extrinsic reward. You are unaware of the passage of time, or your own motivation, or other people, or even of being hungry or uncomfortable. Nothing else matters. To achieve this state, the task has to be hard enough to be challenging but not so hard that it is overwhelming. The task has to be the right match for the person's interests, skill level, and experience. This idea is consistent with Martin Seligman's observation that happy people are the ones who have found and exploited their "signature strengths." Csikszentmihalyi's flow can be readily observed in any small child who is engrossed in a task he set for himself, even if it's just digging holes in the sand:

When I was down beside the sea
A wooden spade they gave to me
To dig the sandy shore.

My holes were empty like a cup.
In every hole the sea came up
Till it could come no more.

—Robert Louis Stevenson, *A Child's Garden of Verses*

(Speaking of beaches and play, Isaac Newton, the greatest scientist who ever lived, had this to say: "I do not know what I may appear to the world, but to myself I seem to have been only like a boy playing on the seashore, and diverting myself in now and then finding a smoother pebble or a prettier shell than ordinary, whilst the great ocean of truth lay all undiscovered before me.")

The Harvard lecturer Tal Ben-Shahar has identified four ways that adults relate to the pursuit of happiness. The "rat racer" is miserable now, working hard at tasks set by others that cause stress and are not fulfilling. He or she recognizes the situation but hopes that tolerating misery today will set the stage for happiness in the future. Career milestones are reached but somehow that happy future never seems to come. Harvard has its share of rat racers. The "hedonist" looks for sensory pleasure now and finds it, often at a very great cost to future happiness. His temporary pleasures are ultimately disappointing. The "nihilist" has given up on happiness, either now or later. The nihilist claims that happiness is impossible. Finally, the "happy adult" works at tasks that are satisfying now, and that will probably also bring more rewards in the future. It sounds simple, doesn't it? You have to discover for yourself what those tasks are.

Csikszentmihalyi's and Ben-Shahar's ideas remind us of the proverb, "The gods do not deduct from man's allotted span the hours spent in fishing." While fishing, you are unaware of the passage of time. Fishing may seem simple and boring to nonfishers, but anyone who fishes regularly knows otherwise. Plus, fishing sometimes gets you a fresh seafood dinner. The thesis of this book is that working on your project, if it's a project you chose and that's right for you, can be as rewarding as fishing, or more so. That's saying a lot. More than 350 years ago Izaak Walton wrote:

> And for that, I shall tell you, that in ancient times a debate hath arisen, and it remains yet unresolved: whether the happiness of man in this world doth consist more in contemplation or action?

121

Concerning which some have endeavored to maintain their opinion of the first; by saying, that the nearer we mortals come to God by way of imitation, the more happy we are. And they say that God enjoys himself only by a contemplation of his own infiniteness, eternity, power, and goodness, and the like. And upon this ground, many cloisteral men of great learning and devotion prefer contemplation before action. And many of the fathers seem to approve this opinion, as may appear in their commentaries upon the words of our Saviour to Martha (Luke 10.41, 42).

And on the contrary, there want not men of equal authority and credit, that prefer action to be the more excellent; as namely, experiments in physic, and the application of it, both for the ease and prolongation of man's life; by which each man is enabled to act and do good to others, either to serve his country or do good to particular persons: and they say also that action is doctrinal, and teaches both art and virtue, and is a maintainer of human society; and for these, and other like reasons, to be preferred before contemplation.

Concerning which two opinions, I shall forbear to add a third, by declaring my own: and rest myself contented in telling you, my very worthy friend, that both these meet together, and do most properly belong to the most honest, ingenious, quiet, and harmless art of angling.

—Izaak Walton, *The Compleat Angler*

Henry David Thoreau said it more succinctly in *Walden*: "Time is but the stream I go a-fishing in."

Abraham Maslow is known today for his concept of a "hierarchy of needs." The hierarchy is sometimes represented as a pyramid, although Maslow didn't use that graphic. At the bottom of Maslow's hierarchy are the purely physiological human needs without which we would all die: food, water, sleep, air, etc. If those kinds of needs are not being met, any higher-order discussion of what makes life fulfilling is moot. Just above those needs are requirements for safety and security: freedom from personal violence, bullying, theft, tyranny, and disasters, access to health care, a modicum of financial and family stability, and job security. We don't necessarily die without these but too much insecurity causes stress and unhappiness. The third layer represents our need for friendships, family, love, and sexual intimacy.

People who have mostly fulfilled the needs discussed above are motivated by the top two layers of the pyramid, which are called "esteem" and "self-actualization." Esteem means that we all want to feel respected and valued by others, and to have a healthy sense of self-respect. Our activities, including professional work and hobbies, help support this need. "Self-actualization", the pointy top of the pyramid, refers to the individual's realizing his or her full potential. Having projects like the ones described in this book will go a long way toward meeting these highest-level human needs. Projects can also help in unexpected ways with the more fundamental needs. Dewey Livingston was able to turn his amateur work as a historian into paid work. The Langs met each other and fell in love in part because they were both collectors of plastic debris on beaches.

. . . .

Profile: Charlotte Torgovitsky, native plant propagator

The California Native Plant Society (CNPS) is exceptional in the way that both professionals and amateurs contribute to everything the society does. There are employees of government agencies and conservation organizations among its members, but unpaid volunteers occupy the highest ranks, both in the offices they hold and in their levels of expertise. Other scientific societies should be like this. When it comes to native plants, there is no substitute for walking around in the field. Native plants are sometimes uncommon, small, and hidden. It takes time to find them and lots of time to learn their ways. Professional botanists don't always spend as much time in the field as they would like. My area has over two thousand species of plants, about 1,600 of which are native. Half of the county is public land and all that land has plants on it, so our chapter of the CNPS has a lot to do. Here's what is happening from a monthly newsletter:

The chapter meeting features a speaker on California's manzanitas. These are large shrubs and small trees, admired for their hard red bark that looks like it's been sanded and polished. They're very photogenic. Many Californians know manzanita, Spanish for "little apple," but who knew there are a hundred species? This talk is preceded by a field trip earlier in the day with the speaker to see some manzanitas, and then dinner at a restaurant.

There is an announcement of a sudden oak death syndrome "sod blitz," in which volunteers perform a soil sampling survey under the supervision of the University of California at Berkeley, looking for the pathogen which is killing our oaks. The regular "Third Thursday Weeders" will meet near the Point Reyes lighthouse. There are work days to propagate native plants.

There is a field trip to an area called Carson Falls and a Calypso Orchid hunt at Rock Springs. There are workshops on rare plant survey protocols, plant family identification, viewing spring wildflowers of the eastern Mojave Desert, and monitoring plant populations.

Our rare plant committee chairperson writes a column called "Plants of the Month." This particular month's column is about two species of native morning glories, their subspecies, and where you can see them. There are also the kinds of items you find in any volunteer organization's newsletter: a president's message, an announcement of some student scholarships, a board meeting, a plant sale, a call for articles, a profile of a member, a membership application form, a lists of contacts and events, and a couple of locally written books for sale.

Charlotte Torgovitsky is the president of this chapter. She doesn't just study native plants, she grows them—lots of them. Charlotte founded the all-volunteer Home Ground Habitat Nursery in a space lent to her by a commercial plant nursery. She approached the commercial nursery and pitched her idea. Volunteers propagate native plants there, and hold plant sales. The plants they grow are distributed for restoration projects and gardens to municipalities, schools, and nonprofit organizations like the Audubon Society. There is a project underway to restore Pine Point, on Marin Municipal Water District land. The North Bay Watershed Association, Point Blue Conservation Science, and local teachers and students are also helping. The idea is to clear the area of non-native pines and Scotch broom and plant oaks, big leaf maples, buckeyes, grasses, and perennials, with a focus on berries eaten by migrating birds. Part of the motivation for projects like these is to improve habitat for native animals. While I was interviewing Charlotte, someone from the Marin County Bicycle Coalition came to pick up some plants for a trail restoration project. Charlotte and the CNPS are looking for a permanent space for their plant propagation efforts.

It's a challenge getting "difficult" plants to grow. If you want to propagate tomatoes, you can read a book on it or take a class. For uncommon native species, Charlotte and her colleagues have to use trial-and-error, and keep notes on what works because sometimes nobody else knows how. She recently potted some tiny bulbs of the lily *Triteleia laxa* that she started from seed; it will take years before they are big enough to sell. Many native plants take months to germinate, years to grow a taproot. Some seeds only germinate after a fire; she has to soak them with special paper impregnated with smoke chemicals to get them started. Some seeds have to be scarified (cut) or refrigerated for a long time. Charlotte always researches what's already been done for a particular species, but she says a lot of the detail is lacking in the literature on this subject.

Charlotte is developing her own property into a native plants and wildlife habitat garden. It was featured in a book by Nancy Bauer, *The California Wildlife Habitat Garden* (University of California Press.) Charlotte has also written an article about it in *Fremontia*, the statewide journal of the California Native Plant Society. I visited her garden recently. One of the first things you notice about this garden is the way it abuts a big meadow of native purple needlegrass (*Stipa pulchra*) and live oaks, acres of them, extending down a hill towards some wetlands in the far distance. Charlotte's garden is surrounded by areas of wild land, City of Novato open space in almost pristine condition. I heard wild turkeys gobbling while I was there, and a deer was browsing unconcernedly in the distance. Charlotte gets visited by bobcats, coyotes, and foxes. Three species of lizards and one species of frog live on her property. The land was once used for grazing and probably some of the original understory shrubs are missing. She is restoring these shrubs on her own land.

Charlotte's main focus when planning a garden is who are the plants providing for? She says, "Plant for the insects first." This includes lots of host plants for larval butterflies. Birds appreciate the insects and also the food plants and nesting materials. Animals are attracted by the insects and birds. Much of Charlotte's garden has no fence around it. Deer pass through freely, but most of her 150–200 native species are either unpalatable to deer or so well established that they can tolerate some browsing. She grew many of these plants from seeds she collected. We stopped at a native currant with red flowers, *Ribes sanguineum*. "When I'm hiking, I smell this plant before I see it," she says. She hopes to make jelly from its berries next year.

Charlotte was not formally trained in botany; she never went to college. She was young when she had her first child and much of her adulthood was spent being a mom and working as a designer and craftsperson, making hand-crafted jackets and other items for the wholesale trade. At mid-life, she had a moment of epiphany when she reflected on how important nature was to her. Her grandfather had been a forester in Denmark; maybe that had something to do with it. She started taking every community college class she could in natural history, ecology, field biology, and nursery management. She raised butterflies. She approached the Marin Art and Garden Center, a nonprofit organization in Ross, California, with 11 acres of grounds. She pitched a proposal to them to develop classes and programs on composting and other garden-related topics. For about eight years Charlotte was the Garden Education Manager for the Marin Art and Garden Center, a paid position. She has also taught classes on native plants, habitat gardens, and composting for Tilden Regional Park near Berkeley, the San Francisco Botanical Garden, Point Reyes Field Seminars, College of Marin, and Pepperwood Preserve. She is frequently invited to lecture on these subjects at botanical gardens, garden clubs, and colleges.

Charlotte has published articles in *Pacific Horticulture Magazine*, *Fremontia*, and the *Marin Independent Journal*. One of her articles in *Pacific Horticulture* is on the cobwebby thistle (*Cirsium occcidentale*) as habitat. Besides describing this plant and how to propagate it, she explains its uses to goldfinches, hummingbirds, butterflies, and other insects. She has great photographs of these organisms visiting the thistles. She wrote another article for the same magazine on many of California's most famous wildflowers: poppies, farewell-to-spring, tidy-tips, tarweed, milkmaids, etc. She describes the origins of their names, their relationships to fire, and gives advice on planting and growing them. There is a discussion of their uses to wildlife, a motivating factor in everything Charlotte does.

I have used the metaphor of a "secret garden" to describe an absorbing part-time project. Charlotte's gardens are not metaphorical or secret. They have brought her satisfaction, recognition, and purpose, and they have helped nudge California towards a more sustainable and wildlife-friendly future. Charlotte does consulting work on drought-tolerant native plant gardens. The North Marin Water District subsidizes the removal of lawns to be replaced with native plants. She gets referrals, and homeowners and landscapers hire her for her expertise.

Charlotte was amused when I told her I was writing a book on people who live like professors. Her son is a real professor, of economics at Northwestern University. Maybe the apple hasn't fallen far from the tree, however, since Charlotte has multiple ongoing projects, collaborators, and affiliations, and does plenty of teaching, writing, and consulting. The only thing she doesn't do that much is travel. Charlotte grew up in a Danish family living in Bombay. She shuttled back and forth a lot when she was young from Denmark to India, and then from California to Denmark. She has been a citizen of Denmark, the United Kingdom, and the United States. For a time she was officially stateless. Today she doesn't like to travel, although she enjoys camping trips in California with her husband. She sometimes collects native seeds on these trips. She has about 75 species in her collection.

I asked her for some advice to her younger self. "I wish I had gone to college," she said. "I got off on a tangent—being a mother. I would have been a good student. I like to look a little deeper into things ... but I was a young person with a lot of diverse talents—drawing, writing, sewing, cooking, gardening—and an entrepreneurial spirit. College might have helped me find a way to put my talents to best use. I am happy that I determined, early in my life, that I only wanted to do work I loved, so work has often felt like play to me! A lot of people are afraid to fail and won't try. Like with plant propagation, I feel really liberated to just try things, since I'm more interested in figuring out how to do it than I am in how many plants I can produce. It's not my living."

. . . .

Projects and your family

When I went to the Galapagos for two weeks, some of my colleagues congratulated me, but in the same breath they said they couldn't themselves leave their families for so long. In our middle years, many of us have family members who depend on us in large and small ways. When is it okay to do something that's rewarding to us but inconveniences them? Women, in particular, struggle with this. I must admit I felt some guilt when I left for two weeks. It just wasn't enough guilt to keep me from going. The long-term payoffs from that trip, even for my family, were so big that after the fact my hesitation seems laughable.

Small children have short-term needs like food, safety, attention, and love. They also have long-term needs that are different. They will grow up in a world that's changing faster than the one we experienced as children, full of opportunity perhaps, but also full of ambiguity and competition. They will have to be creative and self-directed to prosper. Watching their parents bring creative and original projects to fruition can give them examples for success. Children unconsciously imitate their parents. I've noticed that since I started to write this book, both my teenage children have been writing a lot themselves.

If your projects involve travel or fieldwork, you can take your children along. My children have done fieldwork with me several times in the White Mountains and the Mojave Desert, and my daughter has helped with the stone line and elephant seal projects. She is an official volunteer for the National Park Service, and sometimes talks about being a ranger when she grows up. When Ralph Shanks was writing books about lighthouses, he took his children on road trips up and down the California coast. That doesn't sound so bad for them. Lighthouses usually have beaches nearby. I know a PolarTREC teacher (not profiled in this book) who found a way to send her daughter to the Arctic on an expedition of her own! She knew about a remarkable all-expenses-paid program for teens called the Greenland Education Tour. She helped her daughter write a successful application to it. Prartho Sereno's daughter designed one of her books. My father Richard Wing went to night school much of the time I was growing up, but the way I remember it he was always home. We must have had dinner early enough so he could eat with us and then slip off to class while we kids were doing after-dinner activities. He probably did most of his studying at night after we went to bed.

Sometimes spouses want to get involved. Ralph Shanks' wife Lisa Woo Shanks edited his books. The Langs do almost everything together. Sharon Barnett's husband Kevin Stockmann started an outdoor guides-for-hire company with her. Ray Bandar's wife Alkmene Bandar accompanied him on collecting trips. Spouses learn from each other's activities just as children do. Your spouse may surprise you with a project of his or her own. The point is balance. You don't want to be selfish, absent, or neglectful, but you shouldn't be a martyr to everyone else's needs. If you feel that way, it's time to create some space for yourself and your projects. I travel on my own a lot, for periods of up to a month, but over the long-term I still sleep at home about 95 percent of the time. That doesn't seem so bad. I know people who travel on business a lot more than that.

Finally, all families need money. Most of the people profiled in this book earn extra income from their projects, whether it's consulting fees, prizes, teaching stipends, or book sales. Sometimes it's just a few thousand dollars; sometimes it's a lot. Dewey Livingston's projects resulted in a career with the National Park Service. The Langs earn extra income from selling prints of their art and Ralph Shanks' books have been profitable. Sharon Barnett and I earn money by teaching, on top of our day jobs, which are also teaching jobs. Lindsay Knippenberg, Bill Motzer, Dewey Livingston, and Charlotte Torgovitsky are in demand as paid consultants. Bill Schmoker gets free optical equipment that he probably would have purchased otherwise, and Kevin Witte won a large cash award.

Conclusion

"I learned this, at least, by my experiment: that if one advances confidently in the direction of his dreams, and endeavours to live the life which he has imagined, he will meet with a success unexpected in common hours. He will put some things behind, will pass an invisible boundary; new, universal, and more liberal laws will begin to establish themselves around and within him; or the old laws be expanded, and interpreted in his favour in a more liberal sense, and he will live with the license of a higher order of beings."
—Henry David Thoreau, *Walden*

Anyone can do original projects in the arts, humanities, and sciences. An advanced degree is not necessary. What is necessary is an idea, and a sustained desire to follow through on it. Ideas arise from experience. The projects can be pursued part-time. They can be integrated with regular paid work or be completely separate from it, but usually they lie somewhere in between. Often they supplement the paid work and make it more rewarding. Projects can lead to collaborations, travel opportunities, grants, teaching, publications, extra income, social recognition, and enhanced satisfaction with life.

Living this way is probably not for everyone, though, and even if it's for you it may not be appropriate during every stage of your life. If you are a classroom teacher in your first year, or if you have a baby at home, you should postpone major initiatives until you have more energy. Meanwhile you can make plans. Like the people profiled in this book, you will find that once you embark on a project that feels right for you, no matter how modestly you begin it, one thing leads to another. You will probably surprise yourself with where it takes you.

So how do you get started? Knock on somebody's door, like Dewey Livingston. Start a collection, like Richard and Judith Selby Lang or Ray Bandar, or study somebody else's collections, like Ralph Shanks and

Richard Wing. Apply for things, like Lindsay Knippenberg and Prartho Sereno. Take evening classes, like Richard Wing and Charlotte Torgovitsky. Volunteer and collaborate everywhere you can, like Sharon Barnett. Leverage your professional expertise, like Bill Motzer. Push your hobby to the next level, like Bill Schmoker or John Wade. Identify a need for data and ask people to help like Gretchen LeBuhn and Sharon Barnett. Pitch an idea, like Charlotte Torgovitsky. Write about what you care about, and then publish, like Ralph Shanks and Prartho Sereno. Teach a little (or a lot), like all of these people. Travel with purpose, like Kevin Witte and Ray Bandar. Affiliate yourself with an institution. Have a project that, like a secret garden, occupies your thoughts even when you're too busy with daily life to work on it.

Acknowledgments

So many people have helped me, and continue to help me, along the path of doing engaging, original research projects. When I look at this list, I realize that doing it yourself never means you do it by yourself:

Sir Francis Drake High School staff, especially my principals Don Drake and Liz Seabury, my department chairs John Hayden and Mary Buchanan, and my math and science colleagues, especially Cooper Clark, Lori Martz, and Michelle Lackney.

Sir Francis Drake High School students far too numerous to thank one-by-one, but I will mention at least Josh Abrahams, Cooper Borinstein, Emma Burtt, Alexander Curth, Emily Dodge, Jordan Doering, Monica Dreitcer, Matthew Gabel, Meredith Goebel, Cole Hersey, Kate Iida, Angelina Jimenez-Cameron, Anna Jones, Anna Knowles, Miles Lim, Sarah Melbostad, Sarah Jo Millar, India Neville, Paloma Prudhomme, Christine Quach, Isabelle Sarrafzadeh, Anthony Scopazzi, Tavish Traut, Savanna Young, Emily Wearing, and Elizabeth Wing, each of whom played a significant role in one or more of the projects described in this book.

The Mars Institute: Dr. Pascal Lee, John Schutt, and Kira Lorber.

The NASA Ames Research Center: Dr. Chris McKay, Dr. Kimberly Warren-Rhodes, Jon Rask, Matthew Reyes, Dr. Liza Coe, and Dr. Rosalba Bonaccorsi.

The University of California White Mountain Research Center: Denise Waterbury, Dr. John Smiley, and Tim Forsell.

The Arctic Research Consortium of the United States: Janet Warburton, Kristin Timm, and Reija Shnoro.

The State University of New York at Buffalo: Professor Ezra Zubrow, Dr. Eva Hulse, Dr. Greg Korosec, and Dr. Dustin Keeler.

McGill University (Canada): Professor Andre Costopolous, Dr. Jennifer Bracewell, and Dr. Colin Wren.

The University of Pretoria (South Africa): Professor Don Cowan.

Northern Arizona University: Professor Egbert Schwartz.

The United States National Park Service: Dr. Sarah Allen, Sarah Codde, Dorcy Brownback Curth, D.S. (Dewey) Livingston, and Carola DeRooy.

The United States National Oceanic and Atmospheric Administration: Naomi Pollack, Jennifer Stock, and Dan Howard.

The people profiled in this book: Raymond Bandar, Sharon Barnett, Richard and Judith Selby Lang, Professor Gretchen LeBuhn of San Francisco State University, D.S. (Dewey) Livingston, Lindsay Knippenberg, Dr. William E. Motzer, Bill Schmoker, Prartho Sereno, Ralph C. Shanks, Charlotte Torgovitsky, John Wade, Richard V. Wing, and Kevin Witte.

My family: Katherine, George, and Elizabeth Wing, who indulged me my absences and my writing, and frequently helped in the field.

Financial support from the Drake Fund, the PG&E Solar Schools Program, the Toshiba America Foundation, the California Fertilizer Foundation, the Amgen Corporation, the ING Corporation, the Toyota Motor Sales Company, the National Aeronautics and Space Administration, the National Oceanic and Atmospheric Administration, the Mars Institute, the Earthwatch Institute, the National Science Foundation, and the National Geographic Society.

Appendices

All-Expenses-Paid Study Tours for Teachers

In 2007, I went to the Galapagos for two weeks, courtesy of the Toyota Motor Sales Corporation. We saw wildlife, traveled between the islands, met local teachers, and visited Galapagos schools. The experience made me a better teacher of evolution, and it was after a visit to a demonstration farm in the Galapagos that I first had the idea for our school's high altitude garden project.

In 2009, I went to northern Finland to work on an archaeology expedition. We studied 5000-year-old hunter-gatherers. I learned how to blog from the field on that trip and I learned enough about prehistoric archaeology to contemplate tackling the origins of Marin County's puzzling stone line.

Also in 2009, I went to the Mojave Desert with NASA astrobiologists to study cyanobacteria. That trip gave me some ideas for field-oriented student research like my school's artificial hypolith project. In 2010 and 2012, I went to Namibia with the same NASA astrobiologists. In 2011 I went to Abu Dhabi (United Arab Emirates) with them and, in 2016, I went to Ladakh (India). In 2015, I was a NOAA Teacher At Sea off the California coast and in 2016 I got to study leatherback sea turtles in Costa Rica through a fellowship from the Earthwatch Institute.

Some of the teachers I went with to the Galapagos do this sort of thing all the time, and I've become one of them. There are a lot of similar programs that will send a teacher overseas for free. Here are some that I've learned about them. Since someone else is paying, you need to have a very strong plan for how the trip will help your students learn. Program details and websites are constantly changing, but at any given time there are at least two dozen of these programs.

Science, Ocean, and Polar Programs

PolarTREC sends teachers to the Arctic and to Antarctica. It is funded by the National Science Foundation and administered by the Arctic Research Consortium of the United States. The focus is on science. I went to Finland and Alaska with this program in 2009.

www.polartrec.com

The National Oceanic and Atmospheric Administration's **Teacher at Sea** program places teachers on oceanographic vessels. I was a Teacher at Sea off the California coast. The whole time I was within 50 miles of my house (as the seagull flies), but it was a different world.

teacheratsea.noaa.gov

The **Earthwatch Institute** offers all-expenses-paid fellowships to teachers on some of their expeditions in the field. I went to Costa Rica in 2016 to study sea turtles with this excellent organization.

www.earthwatch.org

The National Geographic Society and Lindblad Expeditions have a program called the **Grosvenor Teacher Fellowship Program**, which places teachers on their ships to places like the Arctic, the Galapagos, and Europe. The purpose is to find new ways to bring geographic awareness and ocean stewardship to their classrooms.

nationalgeographic.org/education/programs/grosvenor-teacher-fellows/

NASA's **Spaceward Bound** has sent teachers to extreme environments like deserts, mountaintops, and the Arctic to participate in astrobiology/Mars analog field camps. I went to the Mojave Desert in 2009, to Namibia in 2010 and 2012, to Abu Dhabi in 2011, and to India in 2016 with this outstanding program. The program is no longer funded by NASA but it has morphed into a movement so the trips are still happening. There is no one website—each trip has its own. If you don't know any astrobiologists to ask about it, try the Mars Society.

spacewardbound.astrobiologyindia.in/home/about-spaceward-bound-expeditions/

The Antarctic Geological Drilling Program **ANDRILL** used to send teachers to Antarctica. Maybe it's time for them do resume doing that.
www.andrill.org/arise

Project 2041 sends teachers, students, and others to Antarctica, but most are paying their own way through fundraising.
2041.com

The **International Ocean Discovery Program** places teachers on the deep water drill ship *JOIDES Resolution* for "School of Rock" workshops.
iodp.tamu.edu/index.html

The Monterey Bay Aquarium and Research Institute's **EARTH Program** brings groups of twenty teachers together in locations like Monterey and Hawaii to develop oceanography curricula and learn about ocean science. They pay expenses and a stipend.
www.mbari.org/products/educational-resources/earth/earth-work-shops/

NASA's **SETI** (Search for Extraterrestrial Intelligence) Institute sends teachers on nighttime SOFIA infrared astronomy flights up to 41,000' above sea level.
www.seti.org/

Northrop Grumman's **ECO Classroom** sends teams of four science teachers from the same district to a biological field station in Costa Rica.
www.northropgrumman.com/CorporateResponsibility/ CorporateCitizenship/Education/ECOClassroom/Pages/default.aspx/ index.html

Dr. Robert Ballard's **Ocean Exploration Trust** has a year-long program for teachers called the Science Communication Fellowship. You attend a training workshop on the campus of the University of Rhode Island's Graduate School of Oceanography learning science communication methods and then spend a few weeks on board the trust's research vessel *Nautilus*. The program pays for travel, food, and lodging.
www.oceanexplorationtrust.org/

The **Yellowstone Institute** runs a STEAM (Science, Technology, Engineering, Arts and Math) institute for teachers at Yellowstone National Park.

shop.yellowstone.org/courses/yellowstone-steam-teacher-workshop

California's **Forestry Institute for Teachers** has been around for a long time and thousands of teachers have participated in it.You basically go hiking around in the forest—and learn to appreciate trees in ways you'd never think! There are several locations in Northern California, in the Sierras, and on the coast.

www.forestryinstitute.org/

Programs in Asia, Latin America, and Africa

The Japan-U.S. **Teacher Exchange Program for Education for Sustainable Development** goes to Japan.

www.iie.org/Programs/ESD

The **Keizai Koho Center Teacher Fellowship** goes to Japan.

www.us-japan.org/programs/kkc

The **TOMODACHI Toshiba Science & Technology Leadership Academy** is an annual one-week, cross-cultural educational leadership program for 16 high school students and eight teachers from Japan and the U.S. In August, program participants from both countries will work together to develop a disaster-resilient, smart community of the future.

www.toshiba.com/csr/education_tomodachi_stem.jsp

The Korea Society's **Summer Fellowship in Korean Studies for American Educators** takes social studies teachers to Korea.

www.koreasociety.org

WorldSavvy used to send teachers and students to Bangladesh, to study climate change, and to Peru. They say they plan to resume it.

worldsavvy.org

The U.S. Department of State and *Amigos de las Americas*' **Youth Ambassadors Program** sends San Francisco Bay Area teachers and students on all-expenses-paid trips to South America.
amigosinternational.org/programs/yap/

The **Toyota International Teacher Program** has sent teachers overseas to Costa Rica, South Africa, and the Galapagos. The focus is on environmental issues. I went to the Galapagos in 2007, but as of this writing the program has been discontinued.
www.iie.org/Programs/Toyota-International-Teacher-Program

The **Teachers for Global Classrooms** program sends teachers to places such as Brazil, Ghana, India, Indonesia, Morocco, and Ukraine for 2–3 weeks.
www.irex.org/project/teachers-global-classrooms-program-tgc

Programs in Europe

The Goethe Institute's **Transatlantic Outreach Program** sends social studies teachers to Germany.
www.goethe.de/ins/us/lp/prj/top/enindex.htm

The American Councils for International Education offers a **Classics summer seminar** in Italy.
www.americancouncils.org/programs/educational-seminars-italy-classics-program-icp

Oxbridge Academic Programs (to Oxford, Cambridge, Paris, etc.) has teacher seminars that you normally pay for, but there are free fellowships available too.
www.oxbridgeprograms.com/teacher-seminars/

The English-Speaking Union of the United States' **Teachers Learning Abroad (TLab-UK) Program** offers teacher fellowships in the United Kingdom.
www.esuus.org/esu/programs/tlab-uk/scholarships/

General

The Fulbright **Distinguished Awards in Teaching Program** is more than just a study tour—you actually trade places with a foreign teacher for a year, a semester, or six weeks.
www.fulbrightteacherexchange.org

The U.S. Department of Education administers the **Fulbright-Hayes Seminars Abroad**. Most of these are for social studies, humanities, and language teachers.
www2.ed.gov/programs/iegpssap/applicant.html

The **National Endowment for the Humanities** offers many summer seminars and institutes overseas for school teachers.
www.neh.gov/divisions/education/summer-programs

The **Gilder Lerman Institute** offers summer seminars at various universities for teachers of history, English, social studies, and for school librarians.
www.gilderlehrman.org/programs-exhibitions/teacher-seminars

The **Fund for Teachers** gives grants for self-designed summer sabbaticals, but not all school districts are eligible. Mine is not.
www.fundforteachers.org

The paid **Albert Einstein Distinguished Educator Fellowship** sends you to Washington, D.C., for a year to work on Capitol Hill influencing science education policy.
science.energy.gov/wdts/einstein/

Some of the programs listed above are administered by the **Institute of International Education**, regardless of who's paying the bill. So it pays to get to know this organization.
www.iie.org

Home Exchange Programs

Homelink International is not just for teachers, but it and other organizations like it facilitate home exchanges between members, some of whom are teachers. Most often it's a direct simultaneous swap: My house for your house during an agreed-upon period, typically a few weeks. No money changes hands. I have done this twice though Homelink, to Norway and to England, and both times had a great experience.

homelink-usa.org/

University Extension Schools and Programs

Boston University: www.bu.edu/met

Columbia University: ce.columbia.edu/

Georgetown University: scs.georgetown.edu/

Harvard University: www.extension.harvard.edu

The Johns Hopkins University: advanced.jhu.edu/

New York University: www.scps.nyu.edu/

Northwestern University: sps.northwestern.edu/

Stanford University: mla.stanford.edu

The University of California at Berkeley: extension.berkeley.edu/

The University of California at Los Angeles:
www.uclaextension.edu/

The University of Chicago: grahamschool.uchicago.edu/

The University of London: www.bbk.ac.uk

The University of Pennsylvania: www.sas.upenn.edu/lps/

The University of Toronto: learn.utoronto.ca/

Citizen Science Programs

American Association of Variable Star Observers: www.aavso.org/

Audubon Society Christmas Bird Count: birds.audubon.org/christmas-bird-count

Be a Martian: beamartian.jpl.nasa.gov/welcome

California Phenology Project: www.usanpn.org/cpp/

California Roadkill Observation System: www.wildlifecrossing.net/california/

Citizen's Statewide Lake Assessment Program: www.dec.ny.gov/chemical/81576.html

Dog Cognition Lab: sites.google.com/site/dogcognitionlab/home

eBird: ebird.org/FeederWatch feederwatch.org/

Great Backyard Bird Count: birds.audubon.org/great-backyard-bird-count

Great Sunflower Project: www.greatsunflower.org/

International Dark Sky Association: www.darksky.org/

Leaf Pack Network: www.stroudcenter.org/lpn/

Nature's Notebook: www.usanpn.org/natures_notebook

Nestwatch: nestwatch.org/

Project Budburst: www.budburst.org/

Project Squirrel: www.projectsquirrel.org/

River Otter Ecology Project: www.riverotterecology.org/

setiQuest: setiquest.org/

YardMap Network: content.yardmap.org/

Successful Application I

National Science Foundation's PolarTREC Professional Development Program for Teachers

Nearly all applications for programs and grants are filled out online, but you shouldn't just log on and start entering information into fields on the computer screen. Read the prompts first, and carefully compose your replies in a word processing program. When you are done, you can paste what you have written into the fields of the online form. What follows are my notes in responses to online prompts. The prompts are summarized in [brackets].

[Contact information]

Dr. Michael Wing

wing@marin.k12.ca.us

48 Redwood Drive, Kentfield, California 94904

(415) 462-6769

Sir Francis Drake High School, 1327 Sir Francis Drake Boulevard, San Anselmo, California, 94960

School Phone: (415) 453-8770 extension 4409

School Fax: (415) 458-3479

School Website: www.tamdistrict.org/drake

Other Websites: www.tamdistrict.org/drake/staff/wing

Principal's Name: Mr. Don Drake

Principal's Email Address: ddrake@tamdistrict.org

[Demographic and school information]

I am male, white, USA citizen

School: Public, 1000 students, 1% American Indian, 6% Asian, 2% Black or African American, 6% Hispanic, 0% Pacific Islander, 80% white, 5% multiracial. 9% are eligible for a free or reduced price lunch.

Average class size is 28.

Total number of students I teach in a year is 146.

School starts August 20, 2008.

Winter Break is from December 20, 2008 to January 4, 2009.

February Recess is February 21–March 1, 2009.

Spring Break is April 8–16, 2009.

Last day of school is June 12, 2009.

[Teaching, experience, education]

Bachelor Degree: Chemistry (University of Chicago, 1985)

PhD Degree: Earth Sciences (UC San Diego, 1991)

Other Degree: Single subject teaching credential program, Dominican University of California, 1998 (Chemistry, Physics, Earth Science, General Science).

14 years of teaching experience.

10 years teaching at my current school.

[Licenses, certifications, registrations, awards and honors]

While in graduate school at U.C. San Diego's Scripps Institution of Oceanography, I was awarded the Secretary of the Navy Fellowship in Oceanography from the U.S. Office of Naval Research. I also won Arizona State University's Nininger Meteorite Award for student research on meteorites. I've written ten papers published in scientific journals on topics in geochemistry, oceanography, and planetary science. A list of my publications can be found at drake.marin.k12.ca.us/staff/wing/Scientific_Publications.htm.

At Sir Francis Drake High School, I have served in several leadership positions: Chair of the science department, Small Learning Communities Coordinator, and Instructional Improvement (staff development) Coordinator. In 2007, I was chosen to be a participant in the Toyota International Teacher Program to the Galapagos, a two week, all-expenses-paid study tour with a focus on environmental sustainability.

[Motivation and expectations]

Last year, NASA scientist Pascal Lee spoke to my students about the Haughton Mars Project, a research station on Devon Island in Nunavut. Its purpose is to test equipment for Mars missions. During his talk he suggested that several of us visit Devon Island and do a science project there. I cornered him afterwards to talk specifics! But Dr. Lee's project has a shoestring budget. We haven't yet found the money to send several extra people to the high Arctic. I thought: "Is there a place nearby that is similar to the Arctic and Mars where we could do projects?" The most Arctic-like place I could think of is the University of California's White Mountain Research Station (WMRS), elevation 12,500'. This summer some students and I placed a cold frame for plant growth and composting experiments at the WMRS. It is the highest altitude school garden in America. Details and pictures can be found on: drake.marin.k12.ca.us/staff/wing/WMRS_ Project.htm.

I participated in the 2007 Toyota International Teacher Program to the Galapagos. It transformed how I teach evolution, and it is still yielding unexpected dividends in my teaching. A participant there told me about PolarTREC. I know PolarTREC will do the same.

[Sharing experience with students]

I teach in a program at Sir Francis Drake High School called ROCK, which stands for Revolution of Core Knowledge. It consists of four teachers and a hundred 9th and 10th graders. Our program is in its 16th year. Our 9th and 10th graders take classes together all morning, every morning for two years. At the end of each year, the 10th graders leave the program. I start each year knowing half my students very well. The 9th graders act like 10th graders right away, so we never have to break them in. There is a "ROCK Culture" of hard work, camaraderie, creativity, and fun that perpetuates itself. Class time is 75% traditional classes and 25% interdisciplinary projects. There are four projects every year, and each takes nine weeks. Most are done in small groups. Points earned in projects contribute to a student's grade in English, science, social studies, and art. More information about ROCK and its projects can be found at: drake.marin.k12.ca.us/academics/rock/rock.htm.

From my participation in PolarTREC, a nine week "Polar Project" will emerge. Topics may include: ozone, PCBs, tourism and development, oil drilling, the Northwest Passage, Inuit culture, wildlife, research stations, international treaties, and polar exploration.

[Sharing experience with educators and the public]

ROCK projects always end in some sort of public performance, debate, or presentation that is well-attended by the greater communities of San Anselmo and Fairfax, California. Often, several hundred people are in attendance besides the students themselves. So here's who would benefit from my trip: four teachers, 100+ students, and the communities of Sir Francis Drake High School and San Anselmo. In addition, Drake High periodically gets visitors from all over the U.S. and as far away as Asia, who come to San Anselmo to observe project-based learning. These visitors will also see the PolarTREC-inspired project in action.

[Submit a sample journal]

August 15, 2008: Today students from Sir Francis Drake High School built an insulated cold frame (a miniature greenhouse) at the University of California's White Mountain Research Station, elevation 12,470'. We planted winter wheat, quinoa, and potatoes. It is higher than any other greenhouse, cold frame, farm, or garden in California. Why did we do it? To extend our Mars Colony Project! Colonists on Mars or the moon will have to grow plants for food and oxygen and compost waste. The White Mountain Research Station is the most Mars-like place we can easily get to. It is bitterly cold most of the year, is very dry, has strong winds, and the air is about 2/3rds as thick as it is at sea level. Students will design plant growth and composting experiments using the cold frame for classroom assignments and science fair projects. Perhaps some day we'll build one for the Haughton Mars Project on Devon Island, in the Canadian Arctic. Our team consists of Monica Dreitcer, Matt Gabel, Meredith Goebel, Christine Quach, Mika Weinstein, Ray Goebel, and Michael Wing. We also saw the ancient bristlecone pines. Tomorrow we'll attempt to climb 14,246' White Mountain Peak!

[Background, interests, skills]

My background is in geochemistry and oceanography, but I'm interested in the Arctic and Antarctic on so many levels:

As environmental canaries in the coal mine: PCBs and the ozone hole.

As Mars analogs: Haughton Crater and the Antarctic dry valleys.

As places for danger, tragedy and heroism: Frobisher, Franklin, Nansen, Shackleton, etc.

The Arctic as a last frontier for development: Fabled NW passage now open—oil in the Arctic Ocean, tourism, etc.

The Arctic as a cultural landscape: The Inuit—caribou, musk ox and seals—our hunter-gatherer past—maybe most Europeans, Asians and native Americans have an Arctic heritage? Mitochondrial gene ATP6.

And, of course, the poles as the regions affected first and most by global warming: Last year I took my 100+ students to see the film *An Inconvenient Truth*, and left with a renewed commitment to integrate global warming and energy issues all of my teaching.

[Outdoor skills and experiences]

I am an outdoor enthusiast. I've led a 9-day canoe trip on the Bowron Lakes circuit in British Colombia. I've climbed California's Mt. Shasta (solo) in under seven hours. I own a small sailboat and sail it on wind-swept Tomales Bay. My family and I hike weekly at the Point Reyes National Seashore and spend about twenty nights per year in a tent. I've backpacked King's Canyon National Park, Lassen National Park, and California's Warner Mountains, sometimes alone. Like all teachers in my district, I'm certified in first aid and CPR. I've led many geology field trips, and I've never had a student injured except for minor scrapes. I've never fired a gun, though, unless you count a .22 in scout camp! And, I've never been to the Arctic or the Antarctic.

[Health/physical condition]

My health is excellent. I exercise regularly, bike to work, and am physically fit. I take no medications except a daily aspirin. I am 44.

[Particular strengths]

Counting graduate school, I spent almost a decade doing field-oriented university level research in oceanography and the earth sciences. Since then, I have spent a decade teaching high school. Compared with most teachers, I am almost uniquely qualified to bridge the gap between the university researcher and the high school student. I know how to talk with professors, post-docs, graduate students, technicians, support staff, and captains and crew, having worked with such people and/or been one myself. I can interpret high school students for them. I know how to talk with high school students, and how to interpret scientists for them. Also, teaching for ten years has made me more intuitive of other's feelings. I am considerate, emotionally resilient, and don't presume to lead when it's my job to follow. I'm not a complainer. I try to make myself useful to others in the field. I have a variety of skills in field geology, oceanographic sampling and navigation, and communications.

[Teamwork]

Unlike most high school teachers, I meet with three of my colleagues for more than four hours every week to plan instruction. There is an English teacher, a social studies teacher, an art and drama teacher, and me. Together we plan projects and field trips for the ROCK program, debrief each other on how current projects are going, discuss our students as individuals, and jointly grade student work. We also meet together for several days each summer to plan for the following year. In our program, we have the following labels for people's roles in teamwork:

"Blue Hat" = the big picture person; the organizer and leader,

"Green Hat" = the creative person with the best ideas,

"Red Hat" = the person who cares passionately about the work,

"Yellow Hat" = the positive, agreeable person,

"White Hat" = the provider and synthesizer of information,

"Black Hat" = the judgmental person; the realist.

We have worked well together for years, and fluidly exchange these roles depending on the task. But in planning projects, I'm most often characterized by the "White Hat" and/or the "Blue Hat."

[Engage students]

We do four ROCK projects every year. Two examples of projects include: The "Art is Everywhere" Project. You end up creating a work of art for public viewing, but there are many steps of research, reflection, and project management (deadlines and budgets) along the way.

The Disease Project: In ordinary school, you might write a research paper on tuberculosis. Here you start by researching your disease, but then you create a timeline showing your disease throughout history. You build an annotated 3-D model of how your disease works in the body. You write an original song about your disease and perform it in front of 100 people. You write several fictional narratives from the point of view of disease victims and pathogens. And you debate 26 other diseases in a debate tournament to see who gets the most funding for research and prevention. To succeed in the debate, you need to learn about the other 25 diseases as well! (Our Chronic Fatigue Syndrome group had an article written about them in *The CFIDS Chronicle*: Young, Pamela. "New" School. The CFIDS Chronicle, Vol. 19; Issue 3, Summer 2006, page 29.)

[Additional skills, languages, information]

I speak passable Spanish. I guess that would only be helpful in some parts of Antarctica and Patagonia. Even before I heard of PolarTREC I've been reading almost every book I can find about the Arctic: authors like Rockwell Kent, Peter Freuchen, Farley Mowatt, William Vollmann, Gretchen Freund, Jerry Kobalenko, and of course Robert Service and Jack London.

[Research location—Arctic or Antarctic?]

Either. Who wouldn't jump at the chance to go to either place? The Arctic, though, does have one attraction for me that the Antarctic lacks: an indigenous native culture that goes back thousands of years. But, not all Arctic expeditions would go to Inuit areas.

[Dates available]

These are the windows of time in which I have no teaching responsibilities: February 14–22, 2009, April 11–19, 2009, June 12–August 18, 2009, December 18, 2009 through January 4, 2010, February 13–21, 2010, April 10–18, 2010.

However, I can take two weeks off, or slightly more, from teaching to participate in PolarTREC. So, my availability for longer expeditions is as follows: February 2009, April 2009, June, July, August 2009, December 2009–mid-January 2010, February 2010, April 2010. Two-week expeditions I can do any time. I would prefer to be in the field two to four weeks.

[Technology skills]

Many people are better at fixing computers than I am! However, while in graduate school I actually did build my own mass spectrometer, which included a digital oscilloscope to convert electrical current from ions hitting a target into data which can be quantified and saved on a computer. Getting these and other off-the-shelf electrical components to talk to each other was a challenge. I did it by reading the manuals, trial & error, talking to knowledgeable people, being patient, and not being afraid to use a low-tech solution when the high-tech strategy wasn't working.

[Technology in classroom]

As a teacher in the ROCK program, I serve as a part-time computer teacher. Other students in our district have to take a course called "Introduction to Computers," but our students are exempted from it because we use so much technology in the ROCK projects that they end up learning all the skills in the course of completing their projects. The students are 9th and 10th graders, so the skills we require are fairly basic: word processing, timed typing, making Power Point presentations, internet research skills, using library data bases, remote access to the school's computer network, spreadsheets, making graphs on Excel, video editing, etc. Preferred operating system: Windows XP.

[Computer knowledge and proficiency]

I spend one hour to three hours a day on a computer

Excellent word-processing skills

I send emails with attachments

I have created content in an online blog

I learn by studying the manual and then trying it out

I use laptop, MS Word, Internet Explorer, email daily

I use digital camera, MS Excel, Photoshop frequently

I use MP3 player, audio recorder, instant messaging rarely or never

YES, I can start a computer, open an application, save and retrieve files, cut/paste text, log in to a website, use a digital camera and transfer photos, create folders, rename files, delete files, use spell check and grammar to edit, create, send, forward, reply, and save email messages, post messages to online discussion lists, do an Internet search, use Instant Messaging, install applications, upload and download files, create HTML documents, and use a cell phone.

NO, I have never used a satellite phone.

[References]

Mr. Don Drake

Principal, Sir Francis Drake High School

drake@tamdistrict.org

work phone (415) 458-3477

Mr. Asif Rahman

Science Department Chair, Sir Francis Drake High School

rahman@tamdistrict.org

work phone (415) 945-3600, ex. 4318

Mr. Paul Grifo

Social Studies Department Chair, Sir Francis Drake High School

grifo@tamdistrict.org

work phone (415) 945-3600, ex. 4437

Successful Application II
National Geographic Society's Waitt Grant for Research

[Principal Investigator Information]

Dr. Michael R. Wing

Sir Francis Drake High School

Science Department

1327 Sir Francis Drake Boulevard

San Anselmo, CA 94960 USA

Telephone number (415) 453-8770 ex. 4409

Fax number (414) 458-3480

Email address wing@tamdistrict.org

Current Position and/or Rank: Teacher

Date of Birth: 09/14/1963

Country of Primary Citizenship: USA

How did you hear about us: NGS Website

[Education]

Ph.D. Earth Sciences 1991, University of California at San Diego / Scripps Institution of Oceanography

B.A Chemistry 1985, University of Chicago

[Project information]

Today's date: 06/26/2011

Project title: A Worldwide Array of Artificial Hypoliths: First Data

Start fieldwork: 04/30/2012

End fieldwork: 07/25/2012

Funds requested: 12,000

Total project budget: 16,100

This is not a dissertation project

[Qualifications]

It is probably unusual for a high school teacher to apply for an NGS/ Waitt grant. However, this Principal Investigator does have a Ph.D. in an appropriate field, a track record of publications and awards, and an ongoing collaboration with a NASA researcher. The fact that high school students are involved in designing and deploying this project is icing on the cake, and it offers a unique opportunity for education and public outreach.

[Project abstract]

Cyanobacteria are simple, ancient, and durable microorganisms. They live almost everywhere on Earth and are not restricted to extreme environments. Wherever conditions get really tough, you find green films of cyanobacteria under rocks ("hypolithic" = "under rocks"). Hypoliths are best known from the Arctic and the Antarctica, but they are present worldwide in deserts and alpine areas. The best rocks are translucent ones, like quartz and marble. The rocks transmit some visible light but block the harsh ultraviolet light that can harm living cells. The rocks also trap moisture and protect the cells underneath from temperature extremes. Hypoliths are of interest to astrobiologists because of the potential for cyanobacteria or similar organisms to live on Mars. Very little is known about hypoliths. The growth is difficult to quantify, since it responds to the contours of each rock. However, by placing pre-cut rocks of standardized dimensions in extreme environments, one can rigorously control for variables like light transmission, starting inoculations, and time. Starting in 2010, our school has deployed artifical hypoliths in extreme locations around the world. The "rocks" are glass and marble tiles from building supply stores. This proposal seeks to re-visit sites in the Arctic and Africa and measure cyanobacterial growth. This project has management implications for areas containing hypoliths. How long does it take for a fresh rock surface to become colonized? If the answer is "centuries," then human activities in sensitive areas may need to be restricted more than if the answer is "months."

[Fields of science]

Biology-Microbiology, Geography-Physical-Climatology, Geology

[Classification]

Biogeography, Ecology, Conservation

[Locations]

Africa-Namibia, North America-Canada-Nunavut, North America-United States-California. Project does not involve travel to Cuba, Iran, Sudan, Syria, Zimbabwe, Somalia, or North Korea.

[Geographical features]

Namib Desert, Devon Island, White Mountain

[Grant program]

Waitt Grant

[Latitude/longitudes]

Latitude -23.5425 Longitude 15.1461

Latitude 75.4312 Longitude -89.8740

Latitude 35.1650 Longitude -115.8079

[Additional participants]

Ms. Kira Lorber, Logistics Manager, Haughton Mars Project, Mars Institute

12345 Capable Avenue, Blackstone, BC V4C 2N6 Canada

Telephone +1 (400) 689-7996 kira@marsinstitute.org

Citizenship: Canada, B.S. Life Sciences, University of Victoria, 2009

Dr. Donald A. Cowan, Professor, Department of Biotechnology

Institute for Microbial Biotechnology and Metagenomics, University of the Western Cape

Bellville 7535, Cape Town, South Africa

Telephone (021) 959 2083 cowan@uwc.ac.edu

Date of Birth: 07/07/1954

Citizenship: South Africa, Ph.D. Biochemistry, University of Waikato 1980.

[Previous National Geographic Society grants or affiliations]

NONE

[Principal investigator's scientific publications]

Ahrnsbrak W. F. and Wing M. R. (1998) "Wind induced hypolimnion exchange in Lake Ontario's Kingston Basin: potential effect on oxygen." *Journal of Great Lakes Research*. Vol. 24, No. 1, pp. 145–151.

Wing, M. R. (1997) "Apparent first-order kinetics in the transformation of 1,1,1-trichloroethane in groundwater following a transient release." *Chemosphere*. Vol. 34, No. 4, pp. 771–781.

Wing M. R., Preston A., Acquisto N., and Ahrnsbrak W. F. (1995) "Intrusion of saline groundwater into Seneca and Cayuga Lakes, New York." *Limnology and Oceanography*. Vol. 40, No. 4, pp. 791-801.

Schuffert J. D., Jahnke R. A., Kastner M., Leather J., Sturz A., and Wing M. R. (1994) "Rates of formation of modern phosphorite off western Mexico." *Geochimica et Cosmochimica Acta.* Vol. 58, pp. 5001–5010.

Sagan C., Khare B. N., Thompson W. R., McDonald G. D., Wing M. R., Bada J. L., Vo-Dinh T., and Arakawa E. T. (1993) "Polycyclic aromatic hydrocarbons in the atmospheres of Titan and Jupiter." *The Astrophysical Journal.* Vol. 414, pp. 399–405. (That's right: I co-authored a paper with Carl Sagan.)

Wing M. R. and Bada J. L. (1992) "The origin of polycyclic aromatic hydrocarbons in meteorites." *Origins of Life & the Evolution of the Biosphere.* Vol. 21, pp. 375–383.

Zenobi R., Philippoz J-M., Zare R. N., Wing M. R., Bada J. L. and Marti K. (1992) "Organic compounds in the Forest Vale, H4 ordinary chondrite." *Geochimica et Cosmochimica Acta.* Vol. 56, pp. 2899–2905.

Wing M. R. and Bada J. L. (1991) "Geochromatography on the parent body of the carbonaceous chondrite Ivuna." *Geochimica et Cosmochimica Acta.* Vol. 55, pp. 2937–2942.

Wing M. R., Stromvall E. J., and Lieberman S. H. (1990) "Real-time determination of dissolved free amino acids and primary amines in seawater by time-resolved fluorescence." *Marine Chemistry.* Vol. 29, No. 4, pp. 325–338.

Gross M., Wing M., Rundquist C., and Rubino M. S. (1987) "Evidence that phosphorylation of eIF-2(a) prevents the eIF-2B-mediated dissociation of eIF-2. GDP from the 60 S subunit of complete initiation complexes." *The Journal of Biological Chemistry.* Vol. 262, No. 14, pp. 6899–6907.

[Where do you plan to publish?]

Microbial Ecology Journal

[Additional relevant publications]

Cowan, D.A., Ah Tow, L. (2004) Endangered Antarctic microbial communities. Ann. Rev. *Microbiol.* 58, 649–690.

le Roes-Hill, M., Rohland, J., Meyers, P.R., Cowan, D.A., Burton, S.G. (2009) "Streptomyces hypolithicus sp. nov., a novel streptomycete isolated from a hypolith community, Antarctica. Int." *J. System. Evol. Microbiol.* 59:2033–2036

[Budget]

Airfare: Round trips San Francisco (SFO) to Walvis Bay, Namibia (WVB), and to Devon Island, Nunavut, via Resolute (YRB) $10,600 requested. Round Trip SFO–WVB: $2000 (Orbitz)

Round Trip SFO–YRB: $6100 (Orbitz)

Round Trip Resolute to Devon Island/ Haughton Mars Project by Kenn Borek Air: $2500 (shared charter flight by Twin Otter. Source: HMP)

All air fares for Principal Investigator Michael Wing

Lodging: Two nights Resolute, Nunavut, Canada, and two nights Walvis Bay, Namibia. $600 requested. Food: One week meals on Devon Island / Haughton Mars Project camp. Two days meals in Walvis Bay, Namibia. $800 requested. Nothing requested for vehicle rental, gas, maintenance or other transportation or subsistence needs, field equipment, or supplies, field assistants or consultants or other field needs, telephone tax or postage.

[Funding from other sources]

Sir Francis Drake High School deployment of artificial hypoliths in Mojave Desert and White Mountain Peak, California = $1000. NASA Spaceward Bound Program: Field support/ logistics in Namibia: Food and transportation in the field was provided to the P. I. = $3100. Haughton Mars Project / New York Air National Guard: Flight to Devon Island to deploy hypolith array: Transportation on a New York Air National Guard C-130 Hercules cargo airplane was provided to the P.I. I have managed to deploy hypoliths in the field on a shoestring budget. Luck, persistence, and the generosity of other researchers and the support of my school have enabled this. Now I need to return to gather data. There are no pending applications with other funding sources for this work.

[Possible reviewers]

Dr. Christopher McKay, NASA Ames Research Center, Planetary Science Branch, Building 245, Room 212, mail stop 245-7, Moffett Field CA, 94035, United States, Telephone 650-604-6823, mckay@nasa.gov

Dr. Henry Sun, Desert Research Institute, Division of Earth and Ecosystems Sciences, 745 E. Flamingo Road, Las Vegas, NV 89119, United States, Telephone 702-862-1347, Sun@dri.edu

Dr. Charles Cockell, The Open University, CEPSAR, Walton Hall, Milton Keynes, MK7 6AA, United Kingdom, Telephone 00 44 1908 652918, cockell@opne.ac.uk

[Project description]

Mountaintops, deserts, and the world's polar regions have a lot in common. They are extreme environments that appear hostile to life at first, but are full of hidden surprises. They have beautiful, other-worldly

153

landscapes, remote and empty. They are fragile environments sensitive to climate change. And, they all harbor hypolithic cyanobacteria.

Astrobiology includes the study of life in extreme environments in order to understand how to find life on other planets, like Mars. Cyanobacteria are of interest to astrobiologists, because they are some of Earth's oldest, simplest, and toughest microorganisms. They live in many places, not just in extreme environments. However, wherever conditions get really tough, you find visible green films of them living under rocks ("hypo-lithic" = "under rocks"). Hypolithic cyanobacteria are best known from Devon and Cornwallis Islands in the Arctic (Cockell and Stokes, 2004) and the Antarctic Dry Valleys (Wood et al., 2008; Hughes and Lawley, 2003; Smith et al., 2000). Cyanobacteria prefer translucent rocks like quartz and marble. The rock acts like a greenhouse window, transmitting some visible light but blocking the harsh ultraviolet light that can harm living cells. The rock also traps moisture, and protects the cells underneath from extremes of heat and cold (Warren-Rhodes et al., 2006). The National Aeronautics and Space Administration runs a program called Spaceward Bound, which is best described as a series of astrobiology field camps. In 2009, the author of this proposal participated in NASA's Spaceward Bound expedition to Southern California's Mojave Desert to study hypoliths. In 2010, he went with the same program to the Namib Desert to study hypoliths (NASA 2010). Many of the world's hypoliths experts were present on the Namibia expedition. In 2011, he traveled to Abu Dhabi with some of the same researchers to study cyanobacteria there.

Much is not known about hypoliths. Nobody knows what light levels are optimal for hypolithic cyanobacteria in the field. Also, nobody knows how long it takes for a fresh rock surface to become colonized, or why some apparently suitable rocks found in the field are not colonized. Cyanobacterial growth is difficult to quantify, since it responds to the individual contours of each rock. However, by placing pre-cut "rocks" of standardized dimensions in extreme environments, one can rigor-ously control for variables like light transmission, starting inoculations, and time. Starting in 2010, Sir Francis Drake High School has begun to deploy arrays of artificial hypoliths in extreme locations around the world. Each of these arrays has been personally placed in the field by a teacher or student from Drake High. Each array is approximately one square meter in area and includes sixty glass, marble, and travertine tiles from building supply stores. They have standard dimensions. Variables in this experiment include: light transmission (3 levels), innoculation with local cells vs. sterile when placed into the environment, average annual temperature, and time. An array consists of 30 marble tiles, each of which transmits 5% of incident sunlight to their undersides, 20 glass tiles with 60% transmittance, and ten travertine tiles which transmit much less than 1% of the light that strikes their upper surfaces. Half of each tile type is pre-soaked in a solution of local water and cells to inoculate their surfaces with local cells, and other half is deployed dry. Each array is located just a few miles from, and at the same altitude as, a scientific research station with good climate records. Using sixty tiles in each array allows us to vary several parameters, and gives us confidence in the statistical significance of our results.

To date we have succeeded in placing arrays in Namibia, Devon Island in Arctic Canada, Abu Dhabi, California's Mojave Desert, and California's White Mountain Peak. We hope in the future to extend this experiment to Antarctica, Australia, and the Atacama Desert. Photographs of all of the arrays currently in the field can be viewed online at drake.marin.k12.ca.us/staff/wing/hypoliths.htm. The total cost of this project to date has been about four thousand dollars, including the deployment of the two arrays in California. That a high school group can deploy such an experiment on three continents on a shoestring budget is due mostly to good luck and the generous help of researchers who go to these remote places. That generosity and good luck has its limits.

This proposal seeks airfare and logistical expenses to return to the Devon Island and Namibia arrays in the spring/summer of 2012 (two years after deployment) to analyze the results. The expense of visiting the California arrays can be borne by the science budget of Sir Francis Drake High School. On-the-ground field expenses in Namibia will be covered by NASA's Spaceward Bound program when it returns to Namibia in 2012. Cyanobacterial colonization is visible to the eye as a vivid green film on the underside of the rock or tile. We plan to return to each array of tiles at intervals of two years, five years, ten years, and twenty years after deployment. In the field, each tile will be turned over and the underside will be photographed together with a "virgin" control tile that has sat for minutes, not years, in the field. Back in the lab, photoshop or a similar digital photography software package will be used to evaluate the percent of each tile's surface that has been visibly colonized by cyanobacteria. Species will be determined in the field using a microscope. No samples or specimens will be collected and the tiles will be returned to their places. One set of tiles will not be disturbed at all until the experiment is over, to control for the effect of these periodic visits.

This project has management implications for areas containing hypoliths. Cockell and Stokes (2006) have shown that hypolithic cyanobacteria often represent a significant proportion of the primary productivity of their ecosystems. Disturbing colonized rocks bleaches cynaobacterial cells when the rocks are turned over. This kind of disturbance is very easy to do—indeed, it is hard to avoid on a desert pavement where humans or animals are walking. When you scuff a quartz pebble with your hiking boots and turn it over, how long does it take for the new lower side to become colonized with a new layer of cells? If the answer is "centuries," then human activities in the area may need to be restricted more than if the answer is "a few months." The project also represents a unique opportunity for science and geography education and public outreach because it was conceived and is being conducted entirely by a typical suburban public high school. It demonstrates that under some circumstances, high school teachers and students can make an original contribution to scientific knowledge, instead of just observing the work done by professional researchers.

[Bibliography]

Cockell, C.S. and M.D. Stokes (2004) "Widespread colonization by polar hypoliths." *Nature* 431: 414.

Cockell, C. S. and M. D. Stokes (2006) "Hypolithic Colonization of Opaque Rocks in the Arctic and Antarctic Polar Desert." *Arctic, Antarctic, and Alpine Research* 38 (3): 335–342.

Hughes, K.A. and B. Lawley (2003) "A novel Antarctic microbial endolithic community within gypsum crusts." *Environmental Microbiology* 5 (7): 555–565.

NASA (2010) Spaceward Bound: Namibia. 2010 spacewardbound.nasa.gov/namibia2010/index.html

Smith, M.C., Bowman, J.P., Scott, F.J., and M.A. Line (2000) S"ublithic bacteria associated with Antarctic quartz stones." *Antarctic Science* 12 (2): 177–184.

Warren-Rhodes, K.A., Rhodes, K.L., Pointing, S.B., Ewing, S.A., Lacap, D. C., Gomez-Silva, B., Amundson, R., Friedmann, E. I., and C. P. McKay (2006) "Hypolithic cyanobacteria, dry limit of photosynthesis, and microbial ecology in the hyperarid Atacama Desert." *Microbial Ecology* 52 (3): 389–398.

Wood, S.A., Reuckert, A., Cowan, D. A., and S. C. Cary (2008) "Sources of edaphic cyanobacterial diversity in the Dry Valleys of Eastern Antarctica." *The ISME Journal* 2: 308–320.

Wing, M. R. (2011) "Drake High's worldwide artificial hypoliths project." drake. marin.k12.ca.us/staff/wing/hypoliths.htm

[Obtained all necessary permits]

YES

[Local response to your research]

This project involves placing glass and marble tiles on the surface of the ground in remote and uninhabited areas. No cultural or religious sensibilities will be offended. Four Namibian high school teachers from the De Duine Secondary School in Walvis Bay participated in deploying the Namibia array in 2010, and they will be contacted and invited to participate in the data collection steps. Although school will not be in session in July of 2012, the author of this proposal will certainly pay a visit to the teachers of Resolute's school. He had no time to do so on the deployment trip, when his time on the ground in Resolute was only a few hours.

[Preservation of study site]

On completion of the project, the glass and marble tiles will be removed from the sites. The ground surface will be very lightly raked. It will look exactly as before.[Sampling questions] N/A. No samples, fossils, archaeological materials, animals, or human test subjects are involved.

Successful Application III
NOAA Ocean Guardian School Grant

DATE: April 4, 2013

SCHOOL: Sir Francis Drake High School

ADDRESS: 1327 Sir Francis Drake Boulevard, San Anslemo, CA 94960

Watershed in which your school is located: Corte Madera Creek

TITLE 1 SCHOOL? No

Ever applied before? NO

SCHOOL PRINCIPAL

NAME: Liz Seabury

DAYTIME PHONE: (415) 458-3417

EMAIL: seabury@tamdistrict.org

LEAD TEACHER/PROJECT COORDINATOR

NAME: Michael Wing

DAYTIME PHONE: (415) 453-8770 ex. 4409

EMAIL: wing@tamdistrict.org

PROJECT GOAL(S):

We will patrol Point Reyes Beach (adjoining the Gulf of the Farallones National Marine Sanctuary) collecting, counting, weighing, and photographing plastic debris. We will categorize it according to type and probable origin (recreational, commercial fishing, international shipping, etc.) and the barnacles encrusting it. We will enter our findings into a spreadsheet and compare them to data from California Coastal Cleanup Day. We will note seabirds and write to some manufacturers of the items we find.

Every object tells a story. We see fishing gear from Asia and Oregon, beverage bottles labeled in China, Japan, Korea, and India, ball point pens with the names of businesses, political signs, light bulbs, shoes. We can estimate how long an object has been floating by the size of the pelagic barnacles on it. This project will become really interesting when the 2011 Japanese tsunami debris arrives. Maximenko and Hafner's model (ocean current) suggests 2014, but Ebbesmeyer and Ingraham's model (current + wind) indicates 2013. (See *National Geographic* January 2012.)

2. PROJECT OBJECTIVES:

1. By March, students will visit the Point Reyes National Seashore on at least six different days and will have picked up, documented, and analyzed < 1000 individual pieces weighing 1,500 + lbs.

2. By March, each student will write a report analyzing the composition and probable origin of the debris and comparing our data set to California Coastal Cleanup Day's data.

3. By March, Drake students will submit a project based on our data set to the Marin County Secondary Science Fair.

By April, each student will write a letter to a company whose name and address was found on a piece of plastic debris in Point Reyes Beach to describe how the item was found and to politely request that the company consider alternatives to disposable plastic.

3. PROJECT DESCRIPTION:

The ten-mile beach at the Point Reyes National Seashore faces prevailing winds and currents, and it adjoins the Gulf of the Farallones National Marine Sanctuary. We will make regular patrols collecting, recording, and categorizing plastic debris. We will identify the species of marine birds on the beach that may be impacted by the plastic debris.

Our focus questions are:

- How much of the debris comes from international shipping, local commercial fishing, beachgoers, the tsunami?

- When will the Japanese tsunami debris start to arrive, and what will arrive first?

- What can we learn from the barnacles that encrust the debris?

- What species of marine birds might be impacted by the debris?

Our school is close to the Point Reyes National Seashore. It's wholly appropriate for us to adopt it. The world's trash (and our own) washes up on our beach. Academic content areas addressed by this project will include geography, environmental science, oceanography, marine biology, data analysis and the scientific method, and global awareness.

4. MEASURABLE DATA:

At least 120 students from Sir Francis Drake High School will visit the Point Reyes National seashore on at least six different days and will pick up plastic debris totaling more than 1000 individual pieces and more than 1,500 lbs. by March, 2014

Our spreadsheet will include the following: date, location, collector, birds seen on beach, item, material, color, condition, mass, brand/numbers/printed text, language, country of manufacture, probable origin, pelagic barnacles, length of largest barnacle, other encrusting marine organisms, and notes.

Over 100 9th and 10th graders will each write a report analyzing the composition and probable origin of the trash and comparing our results to those previously found on California Coastal Cleanup Day by end of March 2014.

5. PROJECT OUTREACH:

The project will be done by the 112 ninth and tenth graders enrolled in Drake High School's ROCK Program www.tamdistrict.org/Page/1073 (an integrated studies academy) and a few students enrolled our Independent Science Research class. It will end with a public presentation to community members in Drake High's theater. Each student will write a letter (U.S. mail) to one of the corporations whose addresses we find printed on the plastic debris. They will describe how the debris was found on a national seashore, and will politely propose that the manufacturers find alternatives to plastic. We will send our results to the California Coastal Commission, the Point Reyes National Seashore and the Gulf of the Farallones National Marine Sanctuary. One or two students in our Independent Science Research class will use this data set to submit a project to the Marin County Secondary Science Fair in early March. We will invite the *Marin Independent Journal* to cover our beach field trips. And, the results will go on our project website at www.tamdistrict.org/Page/6113

6. 4th AND/OR 5th YEAR:

N/A.

7. PROJECT MILESTONES:

Start: September 2013. End: June 2014

September–December: Small groups of students enrolled in our Independent Science Research class and one teacher will make monthly visits to the Point Reyes National Seashore to collect debris and decide on the best timing for large groups.

January/February: 112 students will visit the ten-mile great beach at the PNRS, each equipped with a used nylon mesh onion bag to collect plastic debris. The trips will be between winter storms.

February: Every piece of plastic debris will be categorized, weighed, and photographed at school. The information will be entered into one spreadsheet. Each student will write a report analyzing the results, and mail a letter to a company whose address was found on plastic debris.

March: Entries will be submitted to the Marin County Secondary Science Fair and the San Francisco Bay Area Science fair.

April: Entries will be submitted to the California State Science Fair.

May: Reports to the Point Reyes National Seashore, the Gulf of the Farallones National Marine Sanctuary, the Ocean Guardian Schools Program. Project presentation to the school community in the theater.

BUDGET BREAKDOWN

Budget Item: item, quantity, price per item	Total amount:	Donated Items or Other Sources of Funding (cite source:)	Total requested Amount:
One order of 200 (used!) nylon mesh onion bags (50 lb.) for collecting debris (these are reusable.)	85	20 (ROCK Program budget)	65
Durable postage meter scales for weighing plastic debris (six @ $48 each)	288	240 (Science department)	48
Garmin eTrex GPS (Global Positioning System) receivers for recording locations (six @ $223 each)	1338	446	

Two donated by science department	892		
Nikon Monarch 8 X 42 binoculars (six @ $230 each) for identifying bird species on beaches impacted by marine plastic	1380	460	
Two donated by Drake parent	920		
Sibley Field Guide to Birds of Western North America (six at $15/each)	90	15 (Science department)	75
Stamps (for 150 letters to corporations @ $0.46 each)	69	69 Donated by ROCK program	0
Bus transportation to Point Reyes Nat. Seashore (Marin Airporter or Michael's Transport; parent drivers will also be used on most trips.)	1900	700 (School integrated studies budget)	1200
Teacher Stipend	800	0	800

A Query Letter to an Agent or Publisher

Dear Mr./Ms. [Name]:

Please consider [representing/publishing] my nonfiction book *The Hackademics Handbook: Enjoy the Best Parts of Being a Professor Without Having to Be One.* I chose to contact you because... [Good fit with what you already represent or publish.]

This is the story of a ninth grade teacher in California who learned to do more with the resources he already had. He did field work in the Galapagos, Costa Rica, Alaska, Finland, Namibia, the United Arab Emirates, and the high Arctic, with outside organizations paying his way. He published in peer-reviewed journals, won grants from corporations and the National Geographic Society, and collaborated with organizations like NASA, the University of California, and the National Park Service. His projects range from marine biology to high altitude gardening, to archaeology, to plastic debris on beaches. It took time for him to discover the opportunities that were hiding in plain sight. Along the way, he met other people who use ordinary resources to do extraordinary things. Each new project yielded ideas for another one. Projects made him more creative. That teacher is me, and my life is richer now.

University professors have ongoing projects, affiliations, and collaborators. They apply to grants and programs. They travel with a professional purpose and often they get someone else to pay for it. They mentor others and publish their results for posterity. I have interviewed over a dozen Californians for this book who exemplify this lifestyle in different ways. Some are teachers like me, but there are also other working professionals and retired people. Their areas of expertise include the natural sciences, anthropology, history, and the arts. What they all have in common is projects that started small but got traction. The payoffs were life-altering.

This book has significant commercial value. What people most want, once basic needs are met, is recognition and purpose. This book should be stacked on the front table at every university bookstore since there are several million academics (graduate students, postdoctoral fellows, and adjunct faculty) in the USA and Canada who are never going to land a tenure-track job. There are between three and four million primary and secondary school teachers, any one of whom can do the things described in the book. This book will make a great gift for any teacher. There are several million retirees wondering what to do next. Other readers will include stay-at-home parents looking for projects, and millennials who feel that the older generation took all of the interesting opportunities. It is a business book for the intellectually curious. There aren't any others quite like it.

I am an experienced public speaker, writer, and blogger, with awards, credentials, and plenty of contacts in science and education. I know my audience well. I want to go the distance to refine and promote this book. I hope you will [represent/publish] it. A full proposal is attached. I look forward to hearing from you and to meeting you in person.

Sincerely yours,

Michael R. Wing, Ph.D.
Sir Francis Drake High School
1327 Sir Francis Drake Boulevard
San Anselmo, California 94960
(415) 462-6769
(415) 458-3480 (fax)
wing@tamdistrict.org
michaelrwing.com

Bibliography

Belluck, Pam. "Harvard, for Less: Extension Courses' New Allure." *New York Times*, 18 November, 2005.

Ben-Shahar, Tal. *Happier: Learn the Secrets to Daily Joy and Lasting Fulfillment.* New York: McGraw Hill, 2007.

Brewer, Robert Lee. 2014 *Writer's Market.* Cincinnati, Ohio: Writer's Digest Books.

Brickman, Phillip, Coates, Dan, and Ronnie Janoff-Bulman. "Lottery Winners and Accident Victims: Is Happiness Relative?" *Journal of Personality and Social Psychology*, Vol. 36, No. 8, pp. 917–927, 1978.

Carey, Kevin. "Fake Academe, Looking a Lot Like the Real Thing." *New York Times*, 29 December, 2016.

Csikszentmihalyi, Mihaly. *Flow: The Psychology of Optimal Experience.* New York: Harper and Row, 1990.

Dermansky, Julie. "The Bone Palace: a sublime collection that never seems to end." Slate.com, 18 September, 2013.

DeRooy, Carola and D.S. (Dewey) Livingston. *Point Reyes Peninsula: Olema, Point Reyes Station, and Inverness.* Charleston, South Carolina: Arcadia Publishing Images of America Series, 2008.

Greenhouse, Steven. "The Gray Jobs Enigma." *New York Times*, 12 March, 2014.

Greenwald, Jeff. "Making Beautiful Art out of Beach Plastic: Artists Judith and Richard Lang comb the California beaches, looking for trash for their captivating, yet unsettling work." *Smithsonian*, 13 July, 2011.

Kelsky, Karen. *The Professor is In: The Essential Guide to Turning Your Ph.D. into a Job.* New York: Three Rivers Press, 2015.

Kimmey, Samantha. "Mystery Rocks Draw Scholarly Investigation." *Point Reyes Light*, 24 July, 2014.

Kolata, Gina. "So Many Research Scientists, So Few Professorships." *New York Times*, 14 July, 2016.

Livingston, D.S. (Dewey). *Ranching on the Point Reyes Peninsula: A History of the Dairy and Beef Ranches within Point Reyes National Seashore, 1834–1992.* Point Reyes Station, California: National Park Service Historic Resource Study, 1993.

———. *A Good Life: Dairy Farming in the Olema Valley.* Point Reyes Station, California: National Park Service Historic Resource Study, 1995.

———. *Nicasio: The Historic Valley at the Center of Marin.* Nicasio, California: Nicasio Historical Society, 2008.

———. *In the Heart of Marin: The History of Kentfield and Greenbrae, California.* Kentfield, California: Kentfield Greenbrae Historical Society, 2014.

Lönnrot, Elias. *The Kalavala translated with an introduction and notes by Keith Bosley.* Oxford University Press, 1989.

Maslow, Abraham H. "A Theory of Human Motivation." *Psychological Review,* Vol. 50, No. 4, pp. 370–396, 1943.

McGlynn, Daniel. "Right On Course with John Wade, Farallon Islands Patrol Skipper." *Bay Nature,* 4 October, 2012.

Motzer, William. "Perchlorate: Problems, Detection, and Solutions." *Environmental Forensics,* Vol. 2, No. 4, pp. 301–311, 2001.

———. "Chemistry, Geochemistry, and Geology of Chromium and Chromium Compounds." In *Chromium (VI) Handbook,* Guertin, Jacques, Jacobs, James A., and Cynthia P. Avakian (eds.) Boca Raton, Florida: CRC Press, pp. 23–91, 2004.

———. "Fingerprinting Water (Part 1)" *The Vortex,* American Chemical Society California Section newsletter, Vol. LXXV, No. 4, pp. 6–7, 2014.

Phillips, Anna Lena. "Of Sunflowers and Citizens: How are bee populations faring in the United States? A citizen science project will help find out." *American Scientist,* Vol. 96, No. 5, p. 375, 2008.

Poynter, Dan. *Self-Publishing Manual: How to Write, Print and Sell Your Own Book.* Santa Barbara, California: Para Publishing, 2007.

Schmoker, Bill. "Go Birding in Bad Weather." In *Good Birders Don't Wear White: 50 Tips from North America's Top Birders,* Lisa White (Ed.) New York: Houghton Mifflin Company, 2007.

——— "Amateur Bird Videography." *Colorado Birds,* The Colorado Field Ornithologists' Quarterly, Vol. 50, No. 1, pp. 317–318, 2016.

Schwartz, Barry. *The Paradox of Choice: Why More is Less.* New York: Harper Perennial, 2004.

Seligman, Martin E.P. *Authentic Happiness: Using the New Positive Psychology to Realize Your Potential for Lasting Fulfillment.* New York: Atria Books, 2004.

Sereno, Prartho. *Everyday Miracles: An A to Z Guide to the Simple Wonders of Life*. New York: Kensington Publishing, 1998.

———. *Garden Sutra*. Georgetown, Kentucky: Finishing Line Press, 2005.

———. *Causing a Stir: The Secret Lives & Loves of Kitchen Utensils*. San Anselmo, California: Mansarovar Press, 2007.

———. *Call from Paris*. Washington, DC: The Word Works, 2008.

———. *Elephant Raga*. Spokane, Washington: Lynx House Press, 2015.

Shanks, Ralph. *Guardians of the Golden Gate: Lighthouses and Lifeboat Stations of San Francisco Bay*. Novato, California: Costaño Books, 1990.

———. *North American Indian Travel Guide*. Novato, California: Costaño Books, 1994.

Shanks, Ralph and Lisa Woo Shanks. *Indian Baskets of Central California: Art, Culture and History*. Novato, California: Novato, California: Costaño Books/ Miwok Archaeological Preserve of Marin, 2006.

———. *California Indian Baskets: San Diego to Santa Barbara and Beyond to the San Joaquin Valley, Mountains and Deserts*. Novato, California: Costaño Books/ Miwok Archaeological Preserve of Marin, 2010.

———. *Indian Baskets of Northern California and Oregon*. Novato, California: Costaño Books/ Miwok Archaeological Preserve of Marin, 2015.

Shanks, Ralph and Wick York. *U.S. Life-Saving Service: Heroes, Rescues and Architecture of the Early Coast Guard*. Novato, California: Costaño Books, 1996.

Sommer, Lauren. "A Bone Collector's Basement of Animal Skulls Sees the Light." *All Things Considered*, National Public Radio, 10 June 2014.

Swarns, Rachel L. "Crowded Out of Ivory Tower, Adjuncts See a Life Less Lofty." *New York Times*, 19 January, 2014.

Thoreau, Henry David. *Walden, or Life in the Woods*. Norwalk Connecticut: The Easton Press, 1854.

Torgovitsky, Charlotte. *Thistle Lovers All: The Cobwebby Thistle as Habitat*. Pacific Horticulture, April 2008.

———. *The Untamable Beauty of California's Wildflowers*. Pacific Horticulture, October, 2008.

———. "My Home Ground: Inspiration for a Habitat Garden." *Fremontia*, Journal of the California Native Plant Society, Vol. 41, No. 1, pp. 30–33, 2013.

Tuhus-Dubrow, Rebecca. "The Repurposed Ph.D.: Finding Life after Academia— and Not Feeling Bad About It." *New York Times*, 1 November, 2013.

Upshaw, Jennifer. "Life on Mars: In effort to prove they can grow food in desolate places, Drake students create highest garden in U.S." *Marin Independent Journal*, 4 September, 2008.

Walton, Izaak. *The Compleate Angler*. London: Bloomsbury Books, 1988.

Warren-Rhodes K. A., McKay C. P., Boyle L. N., Wing M. R., Kiekebusch E. M., Cowan D. A., Stomeo F., Pointing S. B., Kaseke K. F., Eckardt F., Henschel J. R., Anisfeld, A., Seely M., and Rhodes K L. (2013) "Physical ecology of hypolithic communities in the central Namib Desert: The role of fog, rain, rock habitat and light." *Journal of Geophysical Research—Biosciences*, Vol. 118, No. 4, pp. 1451–1460, 2013.

Wing Michael R. "Apparent first-order kinetics in the transformation of 1,1,1-trichloroethane in groundwater following a transient release." *Chemosphere*, 1997, Vol. 34, No. 4, pp. 771–781, 1997.

———. "Get a Regular Job and Live Like a Professor: Working at a High School." *Graduate & Postdoctoral Chemist*, Vol. 2, Issue 3, pp. 20–21, 2015.

Wing Michael R., Knowles Anna J., Melbostad Sarah R., and Anna K. Jones. "Spiral grain in bristlecone pines (Pinus longaeva) exhibits no correlation with environmental factors." *Trees—Structure and Function*, Vol. 28, No. 2, pp. 487–491, 2014.

Wing, Michael R., Iida, Kate, and Emily Wearing. "Stone-by-Stone Metrics Shed New Light on a Unique Stone Alignment at the Point Reyes National Seashore, Marin County, Alta California." *California Archaeology*, Vol. 7, No. 2. pp. 245–264, 2015.

Wing, Richard V. *The H. Bartlett Wells Collection of Ancient Greek Bronze Coins: Macedonia and Thrace*. Cambridge, Massachusetts: Harvard University M. A. Thesis, 1994.

Yollin, Patricia. "The Bone Collector: Ray Bandar, who has collected the skulls and bones of more than 7,000 animals and decapitated many, inspired one of the films by Bay Area filmmakers at the Ocean Film Festival." *San Francisco Chronicle*, 20 January, 2007.

Index

About the Author

Michael Wing is a ninth grade public school teacher. He has done field work on five continents with outside organizations paying his way. He publishes in peer-reviewed journals, wins grants from corporations and the National Geographic Society, and collaborates with organizations like NASA, the University of California, and the National Park Service. His projects range from marine biology to high altitude gardening to astrobiology to archaeology. Wing lives in Kentfield, California, with his wife and children.

You can contact Michael and follow his projects at **michaelrwing.com**.